# Budget Alert

## FISCAL POLICY ISSUES IN GRENADA FOR 2022

Laurel Theresa Bain

# Table of Contents

## In Recognition of the late George Grant

Budget Alert originated from the Fiscal Alert production of the Bain's Sisters that was hosted by the late George Grant. On the publication of Budget Alert Volume 2, the Bain Sisters acknowledge the life and contribution of the veteran journalist, George Grant, to national development, and specifically the use of his broadcasting skills and medium to facilitate dialogue on the issues touching and concerning the citizens of Grenada.

Fiscal Alert with the Bain Sisters – Laurel Bain, Gemma Bain-Thomas, and Dr. Janice Bain, used the platform of George Grant's Grenada Broadcast to air a weekly programme which commenced in October 2019 and continued until March 2020. George facilitated the programme every Monday morning on his "Gudday Grenada".

Fiscal Alert was a new addition to his broadcasting, and we revelled in sharing knowledge and experience on fiscal policies and other economic and social issues. George was happy to accommodate Fiscal Alert, as in his own words, "the programme was an eye opener". Initially, we agreed on a twenty-minute feature; but many times were accommodated beyond the time allotted.

The Bain Sisters bonded quickly with George. His matter of fact but easy-going way of doing things filtered through. We looked forward to and were ready every Monday morning for Fiscal Alert in keeping with the theme, "Knowledge is Power and Experience is the Greatest Teacher". George embraced Fiscal Alert as it sought to bring the business of government closer to the people by improving their understanding of government policies and measures in a straightforward and simple manner.

The Fiscal Alert Team is indebted to George for the use of his platform; and for giving us the opportunity and a forum to engage and educate the citizens of Grenada on economic and social issues.

## A Tribute in Memory of the late Sir K Dwight Venner and the late Ms. Alison Phills

The late Sir K Dwight Venner, who served as Governor of the Eastern Caribbean Central Bank (ECCB) from 1989 to 2015, contributed significantly to the development of the ECCB and the Eastern Caribbean Currency Union (ECCU).

Sir K Dwight Venner was a visionary leader, and a strong advocate for the OECS Economic Union, while, at the same time, protecting and defending the strong and stable Eastern Caribbean (EC) dollar.  Sir K Dwight Venner constantly withstood the pressures to devalue the EC dollar. During a consultative engagement, when asked by a representative of an international institution whether the appreciation of the EC dollar wakes him up at nights, Governor Venner's response was: "I do not sleep at nights". This closed all further discussions on the devaluation of the EC dollar.

Governor Venner was a regionalist. On becoming Governor of the ECCB, the regional nature of the Bank was upgraded. After the construction of the Headquarter building in 1994, the flags of all the member countries of the ECCB were prominently featured on the compound. Regional institutions, such as the Eastern Caribbean Stock Exchange (ECSE) and the Eastern Caribbean Home Mortgage Bank (ECHMB), were facilitated along with the development of the Regional Government Securities Market (RGSM).

The institutions were housed at the ECCB Headquarters, and their staff participated in the economic and social activities of the ECCB, in keeping with the spirit of deepening regional integration.  In promoting the regional integration vision, the ECCB accommodated a flag raising ceremony on the date of independence of each country with the singing of the National Anthem, and the display of culture and products of the islands. The economic and cultural display of the islands were reinforced by the institutionalization of Island Night.

The performance of the Grenadian contingent at the Bank was of added interest to Sir K Dwight Venner.  Governor Venner was a proud student of the Grenada Boys Secondary School (GBSS), so the display of Grenadian talents and culture had to be upscaled. On one of the Island Nights, the Grenadian contingent displayed the economic, political and social life in Grenada in a medley of songs and dances,  with the songs featuring memorable lyrics of: 'When you see me in the cold mountain, what a planting…; Island in the sun with beautiful beaches and lovely people…; We shall never let our leader fall…; Forward march against imperialism…; and Dry weather house doh worth a cent….' With Arthur Campbell, a currently well-known entrepreneur, as the guitarist, the performance climaxed with the singing of the song with the lyrics: I must go back, my little island is calling me, by the now Honourable Lenox Andrews.

This was followed by the sharing of oil down from a big iron pot which was brought up from Grenada specifically for the cooking of the oil down. The now Honourable Dennis Cornwall efficiently managed the cooking of the oil down, a dish which became famous at the ECCB.  On another occasion, the Grenadian contingent imported the talent in the form of the late Mighty Defender who sang about the stability of the EC dollar. With the experiences of regionalism, it is hoped that the Ministers of Government who were part of the process would continue to push for the strengthening of the OECS Economic Union.

Sir K Dwight Venner was an ardent researcher and with the support of the late Ms. Alison Phills, the ECCB librarian, a first-class library was developed at the ECCB. Ms. Phills, with the support of the library staff, meticulously sourced, recorded and organized the documents in the library; managed the collection of scholarly journals; sourced the newspapers from each member country of the ECCB; managed the exchange of documents with the staff of the Bank; archived the historical records; and embraced the move to the electronic platforms. Based on her interactions, Ms. Phills was concerned about the information gap that existed on the ECCB. This motivated her to publish the first book on the history of the ECCB entitled 'The Eastern Caribbean Central Bank: Some Key Historical Facts', which was launched on 21$^{st}$ February 2019.

The gathering of information and the sharing of knowledge were common to Sir K Dwight Venner and Ms. Alison Phills. On request, Ms. Phills organized Governor Venner's quiet research time in the library. Thereafter, Governor Venner and Ms. Phills would converse as they shared some commonalities namely, the interest in information, the same birthday of 21$^{st}$ January, and the same nationality of St Vincent and the Grenadines.

May the legacy of Sir K Dwight Venner and Ms. Alison Phills live on.

By Ms. Laurel Bain who served at the ECCB for over twenty-five years along with the late Sir K Dwight Venner and the late Ms. Alison Phills.

# Introduction

Budget Alert is a series of Articles on economic and fiscal issues in Grenada, emanating from the national budgets. In Grenada, and in the other countries of the Eastern Caribbean Currency Union (ECCU), fiscal policy is the main instrument for managing the economy.[1] Fiscal policy is generally pursued through the implementation of the national budget.

The national budget is the financial plan for the country and is anchored in the Economic and social development plan. The preparation of the national budget begins with a determination of the available financial resources which are domestic revenues, grants, and loans. These financial resources are then allocated among competing operational expenditure items namely wages and salaries, goods and services, interest payment and transfers and subsidies. Financial resources are also channelled into Government capital projects and to principal debt repayment. The details of the budget are presented in the Estimates of Revenue and Expenditure. The Appropriation Bill, which is approved by Parliament for expenditure for a particular purpose during a financial year, is the legal document that accompanies the Estimates of Revenue and Expenditure.

---

1   The countries of the Eastern Caribbean Currency Union are: Anguilla, Antigua and Barbuda, The Commonwealth of Dominica, Grenada, Montserrat, St Kitts and Nevis, Saint Lucia, and St Vincent and the Grenadines.

   They are members of the organisation of Eastern Caribbean States (OECS) which was established by the Treaty of Basseterre in 1981. They currently operate under the Revised Treaty of Basseterre of 2010. The countries are members of the Eastern Caribbean Central Bank. which was established by the Eastern Caribbean Central Bank (ECCB) Agreement of 1983 as a common Central Bank to serve these countries. The countries are also members of Caricom.

Budget Alert Volume 2 highlights some of the economic and fiscal issues from the 2022 National Budget in a series of Articles. It commences with articles related to the socio-economic context of the 2022 national budget and, in particular, unemployment, poverty and inflation. It includes articles related to the major issues that were debated during the 2022 fiscal year of which the most outstanding was the payment of arrears of pension and gratuity to public officers. The status of government finances is assessed, and the burden of taxes analysed by an examination of the mix of direct and indirect taxes. The financing component of the fiscal accounts has been omitted in the analysis of government finances. As such, the importance and the determination of the financing of government operations are highlighted in the article on 'Financing Government Operations'. Budget Alert concludes with articles related to the 2023 national budget in the context of an agenda to transform the economy.

Budget Alert is a reliable and credible source of information on economic issues arising from Grenada's national budgets. All Budget Alert articles can be obtained from the website https://www.innovativealliances.com/.

See Appendix 1 for the dates of the publication of the Budget Alert articles in 2022.

# The Socio-Economic Context of
# The 2022 National Budget

## Exploring Unemployment in Grenada

Enhancing the welfare of the population is the ultimate objective of achieving economic growth and development. Therefore, comprehensive and regular information on social indicators such as unemployment and poverty is necessary to assess the success of policies for achieving economic growth and development.

In the budget statement for 2022, the unemployment rate was reported at 16.6 percent at the end of June 2021, declining from 28.4 percent in June 2020. The information was based on the labour force surveys conducted by the Statistics Department. The data showed that there was a decline in unemployment between 2020 and 2021. At the end of the fourth quarter of 2019, the overall unemployment rate stood at 15.1 percent. In 2020, at the end of the fourth quarter, unemployment was 18.5 percent; and by the second quarter of 2021, the unemployment rate was 16.6 percent. This is highlighted in the following table:

### Table 1: Overall Unemployment Rate

| | 2019 4th quarter | 2020 4th quarter | 2021 2nd quarter |
|---|---|---|---|
| Unemployment Rate | 15.1 | 18.5 | 16.6 |

Source: Stats: *Mgov. gov.* (2021). Retrieved December, 2021, from https://www.gov.gd/stats

In analyzing the unemployment data, it is important to include the basics of calculating the rate of unemployment. The unemployment rate is determined by the number of persons unemployed divided by the labour force. According to the International Labour Organisation (ILO), the unemployed is a person who is 15 years and over, available to work within two weeks and actively sought employment at some time during the last four weeks or has already found a job that starts within the next three months. Therefore, there would be persons who are capable of working, but have not been actively seeking employment and would not be included in the analysis of the unemployed. The labour force, also known as the economically active population, as defined by the International Labour Organisation (ILO) is the sum of the number of persons employed and the number of persons unemployed. This means that persons who are capable of working, but have not been actively seeking employment are not included in the unemployed and therefore not included in the labour force. The application of the concepts in the survey is consistent with international standards and is necessary for international comparisons. However, there is a segment of the population that is capable of working but is outside the analysis of the labour market situation. For policy purposes, it is important to investigate and report on the size and characteristics of that segment of the population.

Along with the overall unemployment rate, an analysis of unemployment by age and sex is needed to obtain a more comprehensive picture of the unemployment situation. A disaggregation of the overall unemployment rate by age shows high unemployment among the youth. In 2019 and 2020, at the end of the fourth quarter, unemployment among youths stood at 29.6 percent and 39.5 percent respectively. By the end of the second quarter of 2021, youth unemployment was 38.6 percent. In targeting policies, consideration must be given to the high and chronic unemployment among the youths. The rate of unemployment among the youths is highlighted in the following table:

### Table 2: Unemployment by Age in Percentage

|  | 2019 4th quarter | 2020 4th quarter | 2021 2nd quarter |
|---|---|---|---|
| 15-24 | 29.6 | 39.5 | 38.6 |
| 25-64 | 11.9 | 15.1 | 13.5 |

Source: *Stats: Mgov.* gov. (2021). Retrieved December, 2021, from https://www.gov.gd/stats

The disaggregation of unemployment by sex showed higher unemployment rates for females, when compared with the overall unemployment rate. The unemployment rate among females converged to an average of 19.8 percent over the three years, accounting for 18.3 percent in 2019, 21.6 percent in 2020, and 19.5 at the end of the second quarter of 2021, as depicted in the following table:

### Table 3: Unemployment by Sex in Percentage

|  | 2019 4th quarter | 2020 4th quarter | 2021 2nd quarter |
|---|---|---|---|
| Male | 12.5 | 15.9 | 14.2 |
| Female | 18.3 | 21.6 | 19.5 |

Source: *Stats: Mgov.* gov. (2021). Retrieved December, 2021, from https://www.gov.gd/stats

A cross tabulation of the unemployment rates by sex and age highlighted high youth unemployment (15-24 years) in females, particularly in 2021. For the years 2019 to 2021, the unemployment among the youth was distributed among males and females as follows: in 2019 males were 20.4 percent and females were 40.3 percent. In 2020, males were 40.9 percent and females were 37.8 percent. By the second quarter of 2021, female youth unemployment stood at 42 percent and males at 36.2 percent.

It is important to show the distribution of unemployment among the parishes and the rate for Carriacou and Petit Martinique. However, this disaggregation of the unemployment data, if publicly available, was hindered by the inability to continue to access the labour force data from the website where the labour force information was originally sourced.

In summary, based on the labour force surveys, the overall rate of unemployment declined between 2020 and 2021. By the second quarter of 2021, the unemployment rate was 16.6 percent. However, the unemployment situation was characterized by higher rate of unemployment among women (19.5 percent) and high youth unemployment (38.6 percent). The segment of the population that is capable of working, but not actively seeking employment is not included in the analysis of the labour market situation. Consistent with the standard ILO definitions, they are not classified as unemployed and are not included in the labour force. Analysis of the characteristics of this segment of the population is also needed for targeting public policies.

The publication of a 'Social Indicators' Bulletin', which provides disaggregated information on the labour force and poverty, would allow for an assessment of the impact of policies on the welfare of the population.

Knowledge is power and Experience is the greatest teacher.

## Exploring Poverty in Grenada – Part 1

Enhancing the welfare of the population is the ultimate objective of achieving economic growth and development. In this regard, the poverty rate is the most commonly used indicator to assess the welfare of the population. In the budget statement for 2022, the poverty rate was reported at 25 percent in 2018/2019 and was estimated to have declined from 37.7 percent in 2008/2009. This information was sourced from the "Grenada Survey of Living Conditions and Household Budget Survey" (SLCHBS).

According to the Report, the survey is undertaken every 10 years. It is obvious that a ten (10) years period is too long a gap in assessing poverty if policies are to be targeted at elevating the poor out of poverty. Also, in presenting information on social indicators, particularly on unemployment and poverty, the data should be disaggregated by age, sex, a combination of age and sex, and by parish to provide a full picture of the situation. It is this deep disaggregation of the data that is needed for the public to understand the situation in communities, parishes and in the country.

The ten (10) years interval in undertaking the poverty survey also leaves a mental gap in the public as to what was the level of poverty during the interim period of 2008/2009 and 2018/2019. During this period, the economy was affected by the financial and economic crisis of 2008 and 2009, economic recovery was slow between 2011 and 2013. Thereafter, the economy recorded strong growth between 2014 and 2018, but this was accompanied by the structural adjustment programme. In this context, poverty was estimated to have declined from 37.7 percent in 2008/2009 to 25 percent in 2018/2019.

Using the "Grenada Survey of Living Conditions and Household Budget Survey" (SLCHBS) as the reference, a rudimentary estimation is undertaken of the possible poverty situation during the ten years interim period. In the SLCHBS Report, reference is made to two indicators used to measure poverty namely, income or consumption.

In the case of Grenada, the consumption indicator was used to measure poverty. A survey of household consumption expenditure was undertaken to calculate this consumption-based poverty with a sample of 1,689 households. Consumption expenditure was classified into the categories of food, non-food, imputed housing rent, and consumption of durable goods: estimated vehicle consumption. A level of welfare, and in this case, consumption expenditure of EC$6,782 per year per person at 2019 prices, was established. This level of consumption expenditure, of EC$6,782 per year per person, is defined as the poverty line. It separates the poor from the rest of the population and represents "a monetary measure of the minimum annual consumption, in dollar terms, that is needed to meet the basic food and non-food requirements of an average adult, at prevailing prices." (Final Report-Country Poverty Assessment: Grenada, Carriacou and Petit Martinique, Volume 1 – Main Report; 2007/2008). The survey is based on household consumption expenditure which is derived by using a fixed adult equivalent weight for the population by age and sex.

The use of consumption expenditure is the monetary definition of poverty. Based on this consumption expenditure method, the "Grenada Survey of Living Conditions and Household Budget Survey" (SLCHBS) reported that monetary poverty declined from 37.7 percent in 2008/2009 to 25 percent in 2018/2019. It also reported that within the poverty group, extreme poverty increased, and the income disparity between the non-poor and the poor widened. The inclusion of non-monetary indicators such as education and health in the measurement of poverty resulted in multi-dimensional poverty of 34.3 percent in 2018/2019.

The rate of poverty, as measured by consumption expenditure, is influenced by the performance of the economy. This is because the income or consumption indicator of poverty is aligned to the method of determining the Gross Domestic Product (GDP) of the country. The GDP is the value of goods and services produced in the economy in one year. There are three fundamental approaches to calculating Gross Domestic Product (GDP), which determines economic growth.  The three methods are described as (i) output, (ii) expenditure, and (iii) income. The two commonly used methods are the output and expenditure methods. In the output approach, the value of all the goods and services produced in the economy is aggregated to derive the total value of goods and services or GDP. The other commonly used method is the expenditure approach where the expenditure for consumption and investment on goods and services produced in the economy is aggregated to obtain total expenditure on domestically produced goods and services. There is the income method where income received by households is in the form of wages, interest, and dividends; and the profits of businesses are aggregated to derive total national income. In a perfect economic situation, the calculation of GDP and economic growth by these three methods should result in the same figure. This synchronization does not occur due to non-reporting and errors in reporting by agents.

It is the income or consumption indicator, which determines GDP, that is used to measure monetary poverty. As the economy grows, accompanied by job creation that pushes persons above the poverty line, consumption expenditure is likely to increase, and poverty would decline. If the economy contracts, consumption expenditure is likely to decline, and poverty would increase.

A rudimentary calculation, based on the elasticity of poverty to growth in GDP and the rate of inflation, is used to provide an indication of the possible trend in poverty over the ten years period. The elasticity is the extent to which the rate of poverty changes as the economy grows. With the SLCHBS as the reference, it is estimated that a one percentage point increase in GDP results in a 1.7 percent decline in poverty. The "Grenada Survey of Living Conditions and Household Budget Survey" (SLCHBS) reported "In Grenada, the elasticity of poverty with respect to growth is -1.71. In other words, on average a 10-percentage-point increase in economic growth will produce a 17-percent decrease in the proportion of people living in poverty."

Inflation is also incorporated in the determination of the rate of poverty during the interim period of 2008/2009 and 2018/2019. While economic growth would reduce poverty, higher prices would dampen the impact of increased consumption expenditure associated with economic growth. During the period 2009 to 2014, inflation was relatively high, influenced by the high oil prices. Thereafter, between 2015 and 2018, inflation was low as the international price of oil declined after the high of 2014.

The 'Survey of Living Conditions and Household Budget Survey' (SLCHBS) was undertaken with a ten (10) years interval. However, public policies that aim at reducing poverty are continuous. Therefore, it would be necessary to establish indicators that could inform the public on the trend in poverty during the interim periods. In Part 2 of this article, the estimated poverty rates during the interim years of 2009 to 2019 are estimated, based on the growth in the economy, the elasticity of poverty, and the rate of inflation.

Knowledge is power and experience is the greatest teacher.

## Exploring Poverty in Grenada – Part 2

In the article 'Exploring poverty in Grenada: Part 1, reference was made to the poverty rate of 25 percent in 2018/2019, which represented a decline from 37.7 percent in 2008/2009. This information was reported in the budget statement for 2022 and was sourced from the "Grenada Survey of Living Conditions and Household Budget Survey" (SLCHBS), which is undertaken every 10 years.

During the interim ten (10) years period, the economy was affected by external shocks and internal programmes. There was the financial and economic crisis of 2008 and 2009 and high inflation influenced by high oil prices. Economic recovery was slow between 2011 and 2013, but inflation remained high due to the elevated price of oil. Thereafter, the economy recorded strong growth between 2014 and 2018 and inflation was low as oil prices moderated after the high of 2014. This period coincided with the implementation of the structural adjustment programme.

The following is a rudimentary calculation of the rate of poverty for periods between 2008/2009 and 2018/2019, based on the growth in GDP, the elasticity of poverty, and the rate of inflation. The elasticity of poverty was obtained from the "Grenada Survey of Living Conditions and Household Budget Survey" (SLCHBS), which implies, that if the economy grows by one (1) percentage point, poverty declines by 1.7 percent. The reverse is applied in this analysis, that is, if the economy declines by one (1) percentage point, poverty increases by 1.7 percent. This rudimentary estimate provides an indication of the possible rate of poverty in periods between 2008/2009 and 2018/2019.

During the financial and economic crisis, there was a decline in national income (GDP) of 6.6 percent in 2009 and 0.5 percent in 2010, resulting in a 7.1 percent decline in GDP over the period. Based on the elasticity of poverty, a one percentage point decline in GDP results in a 1.7 percent increase in poverty, the rate of poverty would have increased by 12.1 percent or 4.6 percentage points to 42.3 percent. With the further negative effect of the accumulated inflation rate of two (2) percent during the period, poverty could have increased to approximately 44.3 percent by 2010.

Between 2011 and 2013, the poverty rate would have increased from the 44.3 percent estimated for 2010. After 2010, the economy was slowly recovering from the financial and economic crisis and grew by 0.8 percent in 2011, declined by 1.2 percent in 2012, and then grew by 2.3 percent in 2013, with a total accumulated growth of two (2) percent during the period. This economic growth could have led to a reduction in the consumption-based poverty by 3.4 percent or 1.5 percentage points to 42.8 percent. However, inflation was high, and the accumulated rate of inflation was four (4) percent between 2011 and 2013, which completely eroded the gains from economic growth. Consequently, a higher rate of poverty of 46.8 percent was estimated at the end of 2013.

Then between 2014 and 2017, the accumulated economic growth was 21.9 percent (Growth rates: 2014: 7.3 percent, 2015: 6.5 percent, 2016: 3.7 percent, 2017: 4.4 percent). Applying the elasticity, of one (1) percentage point increase in GDP leads to a 1.7 percent decline in poverty, the rate of poverty would have declined by 37.2 percent or 17.4 percentage points to 29.4 percent. Inflation was low during the period with an accumulated rate of 1.1 percent which had the effect of reducing the impact of economic growth on poverty. Consequently, the rate of poverty was estimated at 30.5 percent at the end of 2017.

In the following two years, 2018 and 2019, the accumulated growth was 5.1 percent (Growth rates: 2018: 4.4 percent and 2019: 0.7 percent). Applying the elasticity, poverty could have declined by 8.7 percent or 2.6 percentage points to 27.9 percent. However, with the rate of inflation of 1.4 percent, poverty is estimated at 29.3 percent at the end of 2019. The result from the rudimentary calculation approximates the 25 percent derived by the SLCHBS.

Based on this rudimentary measurement of poverty, using economic growth, the elasticity of poverty and the rate of inflation, it is possible to trace the trend in poverty during the interim periods of 2008/2009 and 2018/2019. It provides an overall estimated poverty rate but does not indicate how the poor groups benefited from the economic growth.

In the "Grenada Survey of Living Conditions and Household Budget Survey" (SLCHBS), it is reported that within the poverty group, the poorest of the poor or extreme poverty increased from 2.4 percent to 3.5 percent between 2008 /2009 and 2018/2019. Also, the income disparity between the non-poor and the poor widened. This indicates that while the economy was growing a segment of the population was getting poorer, and the distribution of income was more inequitable. The growth period coincided with the implementation of the Structural Adjustment Programme. Therefore, an assessment of the measures of the 'Structural Adjustment Programme' would provide details of the impact of the programme on the vulnerable groups.

The impact of growth policies must also be assessed in relation to the accompanying employment created. The "Grenada Survey of Living Conditions and Household Budget Survey" (SLCHBS) reported higher poverty among the unemployed. It also reported that 20.8 percent of the poor were employed. Among the working poor, the highest proportion was employed by the Central Government. In relation to sectors, the higher level of poverty was among human, health, and social workers; and these were followed by agriculture, forestry, and fishing. The following is extracted from the SLCHBS report:

"In terms of labour market indicators, not surprisingly poverty is considerably higher for those unemployed (38.8 percent), compared to those employed (20.8 percent). Moreover, of those individuals currently employed, central government employees—who represent 21 percent of all workers—are among the group with the highest poverty rate (24.5 percent), followed by private workers and self-employed people without employees, with a poverty rate of 20.8 percent and 19.9 percent, respectively. By sector of employment, the poverty rate is highest among human, health and social workers, followed by agriculture, forestry, and fishing workers. The lowest poverty rates are observed among the transportation, information and communication sector workers, followed by professionals working in scientific and technical activities, along with Education workers."

The poverty survey was undertaken before the Covid-19 Pandemic.  With the 13.8 percent decline in GDP in 2020, poverty would have increased from the estimated 25 percent reported in the SLCHBS. The Covid-19 Pandemic was unprecedented with the precipitous decline in GDP associated with lockdowns, restrictions, and Covid-19 related health matters. The existing models of the relationship between growth and poverty may not be relevant for this period. It is therefore necessary to undertake a rapid assessment of the impact of the Pandemic on poverty.

In contrast to the consumption expenditure-based poverty, multi-dimensional poverty was reported at 34.3 percent in 2018/2019. Numerous indicators are used to determine the rate of multidimensional poverty including, among others, employment, health, education, internet access, safety and crime, house insurance, piped water, and households' assets such as fridge, washing machine, and computer. This is the non-monetary poverty, but the Report did not provide a comparison with 2008.

These are important social indicators and the publication of a 'Social Indicators Bulletin' could assist the public in understanding the dynamics of unemployment and poverty in communities, parishes, and in Grenada.

Knowledge is power and experience is the greatest teacher.

## Inflation: Causes and Consequences – Part 1

Inflation is a persistent increase in the general price level. It reduces the amount of goods and services that consumers could purchase with their existing fixed income. It therefore erodes the value of money with adverse socio-economic impact. This article outlines the current inflationary period, explaining what inflation is and how it is determined. In Part 2 of this article, the causes and consequences of inflation would be highlighted; and some policy options would be outlined for mitigating the impact of inflation.

The Consumer Price Index (CPI) is the international standard for measuring the rate of inflation. Based on the statistics for Grenada, the inflation rate, as derived from the Consumer Price Index, was 1.92 percent in 2021. (Source: Eastern Caribbean Central Bank Website, 18, March 2022; https://www.eccb-centralbank.org/p/consumer-price-index-2). This rate of inflation of 1.92 percent meant, in simple terms, that the aggregated prices of all the consumer items that were surveyed in December 2021, increased by 1.9 percent when compared with the aggregated prices of these same items in December 2020. This rate of inflation is used as the indicator of the increase in the general price level and the cost of living. The end of year (December), known as the 'end of period', Consumer Price Index is often used to present the inflation rate. There is also the average inflation rate which is based on the average monthly changes in the Consumer Price Index over the twelve-month period during the year. The average inflation rate for Grenada in 2021 was 1.22 percent. (Source: Eastern Caribbean Central Bank Website, 18, March 2022; https://www.eccb-centralbank.org/p/consumer-price-index-2). This implies that when considering price changes throughout the year, for the consumer items that were surveyed, prices increased on average by 1.2 percent in 2021.

The Consumer Price Index (CPI), as the name suggests, is an index. It is a technical concept. The actual price changes, as experienced by consumers, are lost in the presentation of the CPI and the inflation rate. It could therefore be perplexing to some consumers as it does not explicitly show the absolute changes in the prices encountered by consumers in supermarkets and other retail outlets.

The technical nature of the Consumer Price Index contributes, in part, to the difficulties encountered by some consumers in relating it to the changes in the general price level. The Consumer Price Index, similar to other indexes, is constructed from a starting year known as the 'base year'. A selected sample of items, that is, goods and services commonly consumed by households, referred to as the 'basket of goods', are identified and their prices in the base year are collected.  The prices collected, weighed by their relative importance in the basket, are used to calculate the index. This weighted average value of the consumer items in the base year is equated to one hundred (100). In subsequent years, the prices of the items in the 'basket of goods' are collected, and the total value of these items is determined for each of the given year. This value is then compared with the value of the goods and services in the base year; and this provides for the comparison of price movements in the current year relative to the base year. Therefore, the Consumer Price Index for each year is calculated by dividing the value of the consumer items in the 'basket of goods' in the current year by the value of the same goods in the base year and multiplying the result by one hundred (100) to derive the Consumer Price Index.

In Grenada, the base year on which the Consumer Price Index is calculated is 2010. Therefore, in applying the calculation method for Grenada, the Consumer Price Index for 2021 would be derived by dividing the value of consumer items, that is, the goods and services in the 'basket of goods', in December 2021 with the value of the same consumer items in 2010 and multiplying by one hundred (100). The resulting Consumer Price Index of 113.32 in 2021 means that relative to 2010, consumer prices increased by 13.32 percent. However, the Consumer Price Index rose from 111.19 in December 2020 to 113.32 in December 2021. This resulted in the 2.13 points increase in the Consumer Price Index (113.32-111.19 = 2.13); which translated into the rate of inflation of 1.92 percent for 2021 (2.13/111.19 *100 = 1.92 percent).

The Consumer Price Index (CPI), as a measure of the cost of living, could be perplexing to some consumers, particularly as it does not display the actual changes in the prices of the items. Therefore, for the consumers to relate to the changes in the cost of living, the absolute price changes of selected basic necessities in the various categories of goods and services for comparative periods could be published. There are some basic commodities such as rice, flour, sugar, milk, oil, eggs, laundry powder, and other products such as building materials that are frequently purchased by consumers, and the actual changes in the price of these products could be monitored and published. This would complement the report on the inflation rate, as measured by the Consumer Price Index, which is the standard indicator of inflation.

The extent to which the inflation rate, as calculated from the Consumer Price Index, reflects current price developments in any country is influenced by the relevance of the consumer items in the 'basket of goods'. The foundation for constructing the Consumer Price Index (CPI) is the survey of a sample of households and their accompanying expenditure, known as the Household Budget Survey (HBS). The results of the HBS are used to identify a combination of goods and services purchased by a typical household. These goods and services are categorized and placed in, what is known as, the 'basket of goods', which reflects the day-to-day consumption expenses of the majority of consumers.

The 'basket of goods' also shows the relative dominance of the items purchased by consumers by applying weights to each item purchased and then to the category of goods and services in the 'basket of goods'.

In the context of Grenada, the Household Budget Survey, on which the items in the 'basket of goods' was determined, was derived from the Country Poverty Assessment: Grenada, Carriacou and Petit Martinique that was undertaken in 2008/2009. Over the twelve-year period, the items purchased by the majority of consumers, referred to as the expenditure pattern, would have changed and the 'basket of goods' from which the Consumer Price Index is calculated becomes outdated. Therefore, an updated 'basket of goods' is required to ensure that the items in the 'basket of goods' reflect the purchasing pattern of consumers. The recently published "Grenada Survey of Living Conditions and Household Budget Survey" (SLCHBS) of 2018/2019 would provide some information for the development of a revised 'basket of goods' to capture modifications in consumers' expenditure patterns between 2008/2009 and 2018/2019. Supplementary information would be required to include the modification in household expenditure pattern brought about by the Covid-19 Pandemic.

The constructs of the Consumer Price Index, including the items in the 'basket of goods' are important, particularly as this is an inflationary period. The higher rate of inflation in

2021 was global. This high rate of inflation was already projected to persist into 2022 and is now further aggravated by the Russia/Ukraine war. As an open economy, Grenada would not be insulated from the higher prices.

Specifically, the inflation rate in Grenada, and the other countries of the Eastern Caribbean Currency Union (ECCU), is influenced by the inflation rate of their main trading partners, particularly the USA. Among these trading countries, the inflation rate in the USA reached a high of 7 percent in December 2021. The inflation rate was 5.4 percent in the UK, 4.8 percent in Canada and 5.3 percent in Germany (Source: Trading Economics, 18 March 2022, https://tradingeconomics.com/countries). This is a period of political and economic uncertainty as manifested by the Russia/Ukraine war. Prices were already projected to remain high in 2022, which could be extended to 2023. In this context, the inflation rate in the USA is estimated at 8.5 percent for the first quarter of 2022 and forecasted at 6.3 percent at the end of 2022. The inflation rate for Canada is forecasted at 5.3 percent for the first quarter of 2022 and 3.6 percent at the end of the year; and for the UK, it is forecasted at 5.8 in the first quarter and 3.8 percent at the end of the year. (Source: Trading Economics, 18 March 2022, https://tradingeconomics.com/countries). The inflation rate is projected to moderate in 2023, but economic, social, and political developments could derail economic forecast.

In summary, inflation is a general increase in the price level, and the Consumer Price Index (CPI) is the international standard for measuring inflation. The changes in price experienced by consumers are lost in the presentation of the Consumer Price Index and the inflation rate. A supplementary publication of the actual changes in prices of selected goods and services would assist the public in relating to the actual price changes and the cost of living. The inflation rate is projected to remain high in 2022. In this dynamic economic environment, it is important that the items in the 'basket of goods' for the calculation of the Consumer Price Index be updated to reflect current consumer expenditure pattern. In doing so, the rate of inflation would be more aligned with the cost of living.

In Part 2 of this Article, the causes and consequences of inflation would be examined, and some policy options would be outlined for mitigating the impact of inflation.

Knowledge is power and experience is the greatest teacher.

## Inflation: Causes and Consequences – Part 2

Inflation is the persistent increase in the general price level. It reduces the amount of goods and services that consumers could purchase with their existing fixed income, described as reducing the purchasing power of money. It erodes the value of money with adverse socio-economic impact on consumers. The article 'Inflation: causes and consequences: – Part 1' focused on the current inflationary period and explained what inflation is and how it is determined. In this article, the causes and consequences of inflation are examined, and some policy options are outlined for mitigating the impact of inflation.

In Grenada, similar to the other countries in the Eastern Caribbean Currency Union (ECCU), inflation is mainly imported; due to the high influence of increases in the costs of imported raw materials, services and other imported products used by economic agents. This imported inflation could be combined with or lead to domestically induced inflation. There are numerous causes of inflation, whether imported or domestically induced, and these are categorized into supply push inflation or demand-pull inflation. Supply push inflation occurs due to increases in the cost of production. This is normally associated with higher wages and increases in the cost of raw materials and capital goods, which are more pronounced during periods of shortages. These increases in the cost of inputs into production are passed on to consumers through higher prices for the finished goods and for services. Demand pull inflation occurs when consumer demand for goods and services outpaces the available supply of these goods and services. It is often referred to as 'too much money chasing too few goods', thereby forcing an overall increase in prices. Demand pull inflation is generally associated with economic booms brought about by sharp increases in export earnings, excessive government spending, and growth in the money supply due to increased credit and other expansionary monetary policies by the central bank.

In the Covid-19 Pandemic period, both supply and demand factors have been influencing inflation. On the supply side, production costs have increased due to soaring energy costs, demands for higher wages due to labour shortages, reductions in the supply of goods and services associated with lockdowns and restrictions, and disruptions in the supply chain. There were elements of demand-pull inflation as financial resources were available to individuals and companies through the provision of income support by many governments. In addition, the expansionary monetary policies by central banks, through low interest rates and the purchasing of financial assets, increased the supply of money. The development during the pandemic is now aggravated by the Russia/Ukraine war, triggering high energy cost and disruption in production and supply chain. The impact of both types of inflation, supply push or demand pull, is the same, that is, an increase in the general price level; but their resolution requires different policy responses.

The current inflation rate in Grenada, recorded at less than ten (10) percent, is classified as moderate. However, its impact is still adverse particularly if it persists for a long period. In inflationary periods, workers may successfully demand higher wages to offset the rising cost of living, and if this cycle of wage push and higher prices continues, it would lead to spiralling inflation. The negative effects of inflation on the economy outweigh the positive impact. Fundamentally, inflation reduces the value of money and its purchasing power; and the inflation rate could be equated to a tax that reduces disposable income. Fixed and low-income earners, the unemployed and the poor suffer the most from inflation resulting in increased income inequality. In Grenada, inflation would place a greater financial burden on the vulnerable groups such as the unemployed youths and women, the working poor, those on low and fixed incomes, and the poor and other vulnerable groups.

During inflationary periods, the wealth of economic agents, held in the form of savings, diminishes due to a reduction in the purchasing power of money. Also, inflation reduces the return on savings, particularly if the rate of inflation is higher than the rate of interest on deposits. Grenada's published inflation rate approximates two (2) percent. Therefore, for deposits with interest rates of two (2) percent or less, there is no real return on savings. Inflation therefore discourages savings and suppresses the availability of resources for investment. The higher prices lead to increases in the cost of production and contribute to the loss of competitiveness of the economy and reduced inflows from export earnings. If inflation persists, the social and economic impact becomes severe, and it could destroy the economy.

During inflationary periods, there are some beneficiaries. Individuals who have already invested in assets that appreciate in value such as real estate or have contracted loans to purchase such assets benefit during inflationary periods. Businesses that could determine prices and those that provide essential services could register increased profits. Government collects more revenue from the higher values on which taxes are applied and from the higher profits from some businesses.

Mitigating the impact of inflation could be addressed by individuals, the Government, and the Monetary Authority. Individuals should practice the slogan: 'Grow what you eat and eat what you grow'; restrict their purchases, as far as possible, to necessities; and they should use available financial resources to invest. The financial market is not well developed and the avenues for investment beyond savings in the financial system would be limited. However, it is an opportune time to invest in real estate and to purchase equity in companies that are profitable during both normal times and inflationary periods. The surge in the digital economy provides an avenue for investment in businesses that could be profitable, even in inflationary periods.

Government has an important role to play in light of the limited availability of alternative investments available to individuals. The primary focus of economic policies, at all times, should be to reduce unemployment and poverty. This would give the population economic space to absorb the shocks of intermittent inflationary periods. Also, the focus of policy should be to increase domestic production, particularly of food, to reduce imports of goods and services.

During persistent inflation, the Government has to use its redistributive role and adjust its taxes and expenditure to reduce the burden on the poor and vulnerable groups. In Grenada, where taxes on international trade and transactions are budgeted at almost fifty (50) percent of tax revenue ($349.5 M), higher import prices would boost Government revenues.

Specifically, the tax base (the value on which the tax rate is applied) is already increasing due to the high freight cost. Then, the tax base is compounded, particularly for the Value Added Tax (VAT), as the tax base includes the customs service charge and import duty. Government revenues would therefore be increasing during inflationary periods. The additional revenue as a result of inflation is referred to as an 'inflation tax'. The burden of this 'inflation tax' on the population could be reduced by redistributing some of the additional revenues gained from taxes at the port. This could be achieved by lowering the customs service charge and re-examining the goods that are zero rated and exempt under the VAT for the inclusion of some goods commonly purchased by consumers, particularly in the categories of laundry and cleaning products, hygiene products and building materials. Additionally, income support should be well targeted, particularly to cushion the effects on the vulnerable groups, and those in extreme poverty.

With the soaring fuel price, the price of gas at the pump comes under scrutiny. Grenada's price of gas, capped at $15 per gallon, is comparable with its neighbouring countries of Saint Lucia where the price per gallon of gas is $14.95, in Dominica it is $14.89, and in St Vincent and the Grenadines $14.69. The price per gallon of gas approximates $16 in St Kitts and Nevis ($15.93) and Antigua and Barbuda ($15.70). (Information from Ministry Officials on 29th March 2022). Some countries, such as, Saint Lucia have used the model of adjusting the taxes on gas to maintain the price at a targeted level. Gas is a commodity for which the governments of the Eastern Caribbean Currency Union (ECCU) could use its pool of expertise and adopt a common approach to the method of pricing.

With the pronounced inflation rate of two (2) percent and interest rates of less than two (2) percent on deposits in some financial institutions, the return on savings is negative. If the inflationary period continues, the two (2) percent Minimum Savings Rate (MSR) on savings deposits at commercial banks, as stipulated by the Eastern Caribbean Central Bank (ECCB), would need to be revisited. The policy decision would be based on the objective of the two (2) percent administered Minimum Savings Rate, and the independent assessment of the economies of the ECCU by the Eastern Caribbean Central Bank (ECCB).

In this inflationary period, the trend in prices should be monitored and appropriate policies adopted to mitigate the adverse impact of inflation. Inflationary periods would emerge. The best option for mitigating the impact of inflation is to develop a productive and competitive economy with low unemployment and poverty, and with wages that allow individuals to live above the poverty line.

Knowledge is power and experience is the greatest teacher.

# Resolution of the Payment of Pension and Gratuity to Public Officers

## Introductory Statement to the Articles on the Financing of the Payment of Pension and Gratuity

The pronouncement on the cost of the payment of pension and gratuity to public officers by the Government of the National Democratic Congress (NDC) that assumed office on 23 June 2022 has rendered the articles on honouring the court judgement to be null and void. The payment of the arrears of pension and gratuity, and the disparities in the estimated cost, were historical developments. Therefore, the articles on financing the payment of pension and gratuity are published as records of a financial mystery.

These articles outline an approach to financing the Court judgement on pension and gratuity, based on initial pronouncements. The proposal involved the contracting of debt of approximately $350M. The approach was based on the information provided to the nation by the former Prime Minister Hon. Dr. Keith Mitchell in a national address on 26th April 2022. The pronouncement is summarized as follows: i. The arrears of pension and gratuity to already retired public officers is $465M; and ii. The annual cost for new retirees and the ongoing payment for the previously retired public officers averages $120M for the next thirty-seven years.

Prime Minister Honourable Dickon Mitchell, in the post Cabinet briefing on Tuesday 12th July 2022, informed the nation that the cost of the retroactive payment to public officers is about $60M. The Prime Minister reiterated the Government's commitment to honour the ruling of the Court. The nation was also informed that information on the cost of the Court ruling was provided to the representatives of the trade unions, and they were given the opportunity to review the document and submit comments. This is a good beginning for interactive consultation.

The disparity in figures provided to the nation within less than three months is bewildering. This wide disparity could only be explained if the word 'arrears' as used by the former Prime Minister, is different in meaning from the word' retroactive' as used by Prime Minister Honourable Dickon Mitchell. The two words 'arrears' which is money that is outstanding or owing, and 'retroactive' which is taking effect from a date in the past, carry the same meaning. Therefore, the issue is identifying the reasons for this huge disparity in figures, that is, $465M presented by the previous administration and $60M presented by the new administration that took office on 23$^{rd}$ June 2022. The nation may be given an opportunity to understand the rationale for the $465M when the former Prime Minister sits in Parliament as Leader of the Opposition. Also, to be revealed to the nation is the source of the financing of the repurchase of the WRB shares in GRENLEC, which cannot be determined by an examination of any of the Estimates of Revenue and Expenditure.

In the past, the Government has made statements to the public without adequate supporting facts and figures. This should not have occurred in the existing system of governance. The Constitution makes provisions for 'good government'. There is the Parliament with authority to make laws for the peace, order, and good government of the country; and the Executive that executes the laws and is responsible for the financial and administrative management of the country. The Executive is supported by the public service comprising a cadre of technical and administrative officers who impartially serve the Government. There are also defined systems for financial management, including the submission of the public sector accounts by the Director of Audit to Parliament.

The existence of financial mysteries for extended periods is evidence of a **'fatal crash of the system for good government'**. If the arms of government and systems for financial management operate efficiently, the nation would not be plunged into these financial dilemmas. The National Democratic Congress Government has stated that it is committed to transparency and accountability which would require the strengthening of institutions to operate with integrity, and in adherence with the provisions of the Constitution.

Knowledge is power and experience is the greatest teacher.

## Payment of Pension and Gratuity to Public officers

The High Court has ruled on the payment of pension and gratuity to public officers, and the ruling must be honoured. Anything otherwise would be a disservice to public officers. The pension and gratuity must be paid. The issues are how this obligation would be paid, what are the implications and how any potential adverse impact could be mitigated.

Proposed options for payment of the arrears of pension and gratuity must be based on firm information on cost. Even before the Court ruling, technical officers should have been crunching numbers so the public would have a clear understanding of the cost of the ruling and the fiscal implications. In the absence of these, at least publicly, the proposals are indicative.

The Court ruling has created two types of liabilities, namely:

i.    The arrears of gratuity and pension for the public officers who have already retired. This is the public debt component of the liability; and

ii.    The annual payment that would be required to pay retiring officers their gratuity and the monthly pension for all pensioners. This payment would be a charge on the current account.

The two types of liabilities require different financing options.

For the payment of the arrears of pension and gratuity to public officers who have already retired, the Government could consider the issue of bonds with different maturity dates and use the cash proceeds to finance this component of the liability. The ruling has created a debt, and based on the West

Indies Supreme Court Act, the debt is subject to the statutory interest rate of six (6) percent per annum from the date of the ruling. It is in the interest of the Government and the public to replace this debt with a cheaper debt by issuing bonds and using the cash proceeds to pay the public officers. The success of the bond issue would require intensive marketing and networking to identify agents that are interested in the purchase. The power of the State could be used to negotiate with local institutions, governments, regional and international organisations, economic entities, and individuals for the purchase of the bonds.

The Court ruling has increased the public debt which could reach over one hundred (100) percent of GDP. It is important to accurately capture all the liabilities of the public referred to as the public debt. The Central Government debt of $2.1 billion or 70.6 percent of GDP is often equated with the public debt. This is inaccurate. The public debt, which includes that of State-owned enterprises of $0.53 billion or 17.9 percent of GDP, amounts to $2.6 Billion or 88.5 percent of GDP. The inclusion of the debt to retired public officers could push the public debt to over one hundred (100) percent of GDP. The Government should therefore create a sinking fund, where a portion of current revenue is deposited and invested to contribute to the repayment of the bonds on maturity.

The payment of the second component, that is, the gratuity for new pensioners and pension for all pensioners, should be derived from Government current operations. These payments should be programmed as a part of the government's annual current expenditure. It is an opportune time to overhaul the public finances and its management to improve efficiencies and eliminate wastage. The areas for examination are expenditure on goods and services, the transfers related to the social safety net programmes and capital spending. On the revenue side, all outstanding obligations to the Government should be collected. The various agencies of Government should work together to recover outstanding public funds. The objective is to increase the available financial resources which would contribute to financing pensions and gratuities.

After this rigorous examination of revenues and expenditures, and the preparation of the forecasted government finances, then the additional amount needed to finance the pension and gratuity would be determined. The forecast should include all revenues and expenditures, including the operation of special funds such as the National Transformation Fund, established by Acts of Parliament.

If there is not adequate revenue for the ongoing payment of pension and gratuity, after the elimination of inefficiencies and wastage in the management of the public finances, a pro-posal should be packaged and budgetary support in the form of grants sought for a transitory period of approximately two years, while the Government addresses the state of the public finances. The Government has received budgetary support or current grants in the past which average $18.5M annually between 2018 to 2020. Current grants or budget support rose to $41M in 2021 and in February 2022 $81M in grants were received for budget support. Much of the funds received in February have not been utilised and some could be targeted to the payment of the pension and gratuity. Budgetary support in the form of grants is a gift and could be used as determined by the Government. Therefore, as an interim measure, the use of grants for budgetary support could be explored.

Prior to resorting to taxes to finance the pension and gratuity, the government should consider the Grenada Survey of Living Conditions and Household Budget Survey (SLCHBS) report which indicated a widening of the income disparity between the poor and the non-poor. Therefore, the burden of the tax system and the distribution of the burden must be assessed to inform future tax policy. In this context, if the Government needs to resort to taxing to finance the pension and gratuity, the Government could consider reversing the decision and return the top marginal tax rate on personal and corporate incomes to thirty (30) percent.

If additional domestic revenue is needed, the Government could introduce a new tax, but the burden of the tax should be limited to those responsible for the financial fiasco. The Constitution entrusts the management of the public funds to the Legislature and Executive. A transitory Pension and Gratuity Recovery Tax (PGRT) could be introduced, but this should be limited to the income and pension of Parliamentarians responsible for the fiscal fiasco. To the extent that Parliament consciously passed the Act to provide pensions to parliamentarians and the pension of public officers was not addressed, the tax would provide redress and contribute to financing the payment of pension and gratuity.

On the positive side, the Government should take the opportunity to transform the economy as a result of the increased government expenditure and the expected increase in incomes of households. There is a large pool of human resources who could benefit from the increased expenditure and the Government should guide and facilitate the process. There is a youth unemployment rate of 38.6 percent and women of 19.5 percent (official figures for the second quarter of 2021 and which do not include the discouraged workers). The monetary poverty rate was twenty-five (25) percent in 2019, and if the analysis is extended to 2021, the poverty rate could have reached, at a minimum, forty (40) percent in 2021.

There are idle human resources, while there is need to adapt to a new economy. The use of the financial resources should be directed to support the emerging economic activities and to transform the economy. The transformation of the economy requires new types of skills, business processes and entrepreneurs. The Government could facilitate the use of the funds in the targeted areas by providing incentives and supporting infrastructure.

Through these programmes, parents should be encouraged to partner with children and youths and contribute financially to train or retrain in areas that are required to transform the economy.  This could be done in the context of the digital economy, and to develop creative industries, and other areas that would support the reorientation of the economy. Parents could enter into business relationships with children and youths to establish businesses which do not need significant overhead capital to operate. In this electronic global economy, there is scope for employment using virtual platforms in areas such as marketing, website design, data analysis, tutoring, editorial services, entertainment, and other innovative and creative industries.

The opportunity should also be taken to direct funds to address the imbalances in the economy. Agriculture is a small component of GDP and its contribution to GDP has declined over the past five years. The manufacturing sector is small and stagnant. The tourism industry, which has been the impetus to economic growth, seems not to be pulling these sectors. Meanwhile, the food import bill has been increasing. Incentive packages and technical support should be provided for enhancing the scope of domestic production. Individuals could be encouraged and supported to form cooperatives to engage in agriculture, fishing, and agro-processing. The Marketing and National Importing Board should be reformed to facilitate marketing.

The opportunity should be taken to pursue policies, provide incentives and establish infrastructure to facilitate the use of the funds for the integration of domestic production and the innovative and creative industries with the tourism industry. The objective is to direct the use of the financial resources provided to households to rebalance the economy from the heavy reliance on tourism by improving the agriculture sector and the development of innovative and creative industries to achieve an integrated economy with greater food security.

The home is the pride of many individuals. Housing is an area where funds could be directed particularly in the context of energy efficiencies and climate resilience. Houses may require retrofitting to accommodate alternative energy such as solar and for the use of high-speed internet facilities to engage in the new types of entrepreneurship. Activities in innovative and creative industries may not require high overhead expenses and with slight modifications could be accommodated in residential homes. In addition, there are building requirements for climate resilience and there are houses that need general upgrading for which funds could be utilised.

The payment of pension and gratuity is costly to the public purse. However, it is necessary to direct the funds into investments that would transform the economy and lead to sustainable economic growth.

Knowledge is power and experience is the greatest teacher.

## Financing the Payment of Pension and Gratuity – Part 1

Following the general elections of 22$^{nd}$ June 2022, the National Democratic Congress formed the Government. Congratulation is extended to the Prime Minister and the executive and best wishes for their success in transforming Grenada's economy. In keeping with the frequent calls for transparency and accountability in the governance of the affairs of the state, it would be necessary for the Government to undertake a comprehensive assessment of the state of the public finances.

The National Democratic Congress Government has, in adherence to the Constitution, committed to the payment of the Court's judgement on pension and gratuity. This is a huge fiscal cost, but there could be positive outcomes that should be maximized. This article on 'Financing the Payment of Pension and gratuity' is presented in three parts. Part 1 is a summary of an approach to financing the payment of pension and gratuity, the details of which would be presented in Part 2 and Part 3 of the subsequent articles.

In the previous article on 'Payment of Pension and Gratuity', which could be sourced at Innovativealliances.com, the cost of the Court ruling was not yet publicly released, and the proposal for the payment of pension and gratuity was indicative. The information provided to the public by the then political directorate on Tuesday 26$^{th}$ April 2022 is the basis for the following summary of an approach to honouring the Court's judgement on pension and gratuity.

1) The information on the cost of the Court ruling on pension and gratuity, as presented, is summarized as follows:

i.    The arrears of pension and gratuity to already retired public officers is $465M; and

ii.    The annual cost for new retirees and the ongoing payment for the previously retired officers averages $120M for the next thirty-seven years.

The $120M is interpreted to mean that the total annual pension and gratuity, inclusive of the approximately $70M that is currently being paid, would average $120M beginning from 2023.

2)    The payment of the $465M in arrears of pension and gratuity to the already retired public officers could be through a combination of debt, inflows from the Citizenship by Investment Programme and the use of reserves.

3)    The proposal is for the debt of $465M to be paid in two tranches, that is, a tranche of $115M in 2022, to be financed from the operational surplus, inflows from the Citizenship by Investment Programme and reserves; and a tranche of $350M in 2023 to be financed by debt.

4)    The criteria for the receipt of payment could be the date of retirement, commencing with the earliest retirees and those that are ailing and are in urgent need of their cash.

5)    The proposal for sourcing the $115M in 2022 is as follows: i. $45M from government current operations, ii. $45M from the National Transformation Fund or the Citizenship by Investment Programme, and iii. $25M from the reserves.

6)    The Government should settle the other part of the debt liability of $350M of the $465M by either contracting a long-term loan or by issuing bonds or a combination of loans and bonds.

7) A long term highly concessionary loan is the best option. However, few institutions, notably the World Bank, provide long-term concessionary loans. Also, the amount of the loan may be limited and linked to specific projects rather than a reduction in debt.

8) The alternative approach to the concessionary loan would be to issue bonds with different dates of maturity. The Government would need to aggressively market the bonds with national, regional, and international financial institutions and entities to achieve attractive interest rates.

9) The annual average expenditure of $120M could be incorporated in government annual current operations.

10) The Estimates of Revenue and Expenditure for 2022, provides the forecast of government operations for 2023 and 2024 which shows an operational surplus of $108.7M in 2023 and $238.3M in 2024; and the overall surplus, after grants, of $56.3M in 2023 and $188M in 2024.

11) The cost of the Court ruling is then incorporated in the forecasted Government finances. For 2023 and 2024, there would be an annual pension and gratuity payment of $120M for each year; an annual interest payment of $10.5M on the debt of $350M, based on an interest rate of three (3) percent; and an annual contribution to the sinking fund of $5M, which is invested with cumulated interest at approximately 3 percent.

12) The results of the adjustments show that the Government finances would be within budget in 2022; it would tighten in 2023 with a reduced current account surplus and a smaller overall surplus; but recover in 2024.

13) Despite the payment of the \$115M in 2022, government finances would remain within the budgeted overall deficit, after grants, of \$97.9M, as the deficit is projected at \$ 61.1M in the revised budget. This improvement in the Government finances is due primarily to the receipt of unbudgeted financial inflows in the first quarter of 2022.

14) In 2023, the current account or operational surplus, would be reduced from \$108.7M excluding the payment of the additional pension and gratuity and interest on the debt, to \$56.1M with the inclusion of the additional payment for pension and gratuity and the interest on the debt. The overall surplus after grants would move from \$56.3M to \$3.7M. The inclusion of the sinking fund contribution results in an overall deficit of \$1.3M in 2023.

15) The Government may wish to supplement the financial resources in 2023. To increase the fiscal space, the Government could seek budgetary support which it has been receiving over the years. Alternatively, additional resources could be utilized from the National Transformation Fund.

16) The fiscal position, with the inclusion of the payment of pension and gratuity and the interest on the debt, recovers in 2024. The forecast shows a current account or operational surplus of \$188.7M and an overall surplus (after grants) of \$138.4M. The inclusion of the sinking fund contribution reduces the overall surplus to \$133.4M.

17) The Court ruling on pension and gratuity must be honoured. However, the issue of pension and pension reform would continue to be a national issue. The debates on pension and gratuity for public officers

should be guided by the Constitution which is the supreme law of the land.

18) If the Pension Solution and Strategy Committee becomes operational, the Terms of Reference of the Committee should be a public document, and the structure of the Committee should be representative of society.

The payment of the pension and gratuity is good for the Government, better for the population and best for the economy.

Knowledge is power and experience is the greatest teacher.[2]

_______________

2  This article was published prior to the announcement by the Honourable Dickon Mitchell, Prime Minister and Minister of Finance,  that the cost of the payment of the arrears of pension and gratuity to public officers cost approximately $60M.

## Good Government: Core to Transforming the Economy

In the article on Financing the Payment of Pension and Gratuity, the conclusion was that: **'The existence of financial mysteries for extended periods is evidence of a fatal crash of the system for good government. If the arms of government and systems for financial management operate efficiently, the nation would not be plunged into these financial dilemmas**. The following highlights some facets of the system of Good Government, some of which were outlined in previous articles.

In Grenada, the system of public administration is that of a bureaucracy. This implies that the administrative system operates with established rules and regulations; welled defined roles and responsibilities; and documented policies, procedures, and decisions. In this bureaucracy, the Parliament is the highest decision-making body, and has constitutional authority (section 38 of the Constitution) to make laws for the peace, order, and good government of Grenada.

The composition of the Parliament allows it to perform the functions for the governance of the country. It comprises the elected members from the outcome of General Elections. Among the Parliamentarians is the Prime Minister, as Head of Government, who has the support of the majority of the members in Parliament; Also, there is an opposition led by the Leader with the second largest number of seats in Parliament. In Grenada, there is a separate upper House of Parliament, comprising of members nominated by the Prime Minister and the Leader of the Opposition, and it is referred to as the Senate.

The Parliament is required to provide tight oversight and deep insight into the financial management of the country through the examination and approval of the Annual Estimates of Revenue and Expenditure as stipulated by the Constitution; the review of the Mid-year Fiscal Policy Report as outlined in the Public Finance Management Act; and the examination of the Annual Report of the Director of Audit as required by the Constitution.

Then, there is the Executive, comprising the Prime Minister and Ministers, drawn from elected members of Parliament, and nominated members of the Senate, who are assigned ministerial portfolios and other businesses of Government. They are appointed by the Governor General on the advice of the Prime Minister. The Executive, known as the Cabinet, is responsible for maintaining law and order and for the administration and financial management of the country. The Executive is supported by the Public Service comprising a cadre of technical and administrative officers who impartially serve the Government. In carrying out the functions, the organs of Government are guided by the Constitution, and laws and regulations inclusive of the Public Finance Management Act (2015), the Debt Management Act (2015), the Fiscal Responsibility Act (2015) and the Audit Act (2007).

Before undertaking the duties of their office, members of Parliament, Cabinet and Ministers take and subscribe to an oath of office; swearing or affirming to faithfully execute the office without fear or favour, affection or ill-will, and in the execution of the functions of that office, to honour, uphold and preserve the Constitution of Grenada. This is a solemn vow requiring the officeholder to execute the powers and trusts reposed in that office in keeping with the Constitution.

In public administration, good government requires adherence to the rule of law, transparent and accountable government processes and institutions, and an efficient and effective public service.

To operationalize this governance arrangement, the Minister is responsible for public administration and financial management of the assigned portfolio. This is in accordance with Section 67 of the Constitution which indicates that, the Minister shall exercise general direction and control over the department of government, and subject to such direction and control, every department of government shall be under the supervision of a public officer whose office is referred to as the office of a Permanent Secretary.

In this context, the Minister is responsible for determining and promoting policies, and answering in the Parliament on both policy and operational matters. In the constitution, Minister means Minister in Cabinet; therefore, such policies should be approved by the Cabinet of Ministers. By virtue of section 59 of the Constitution, Ministers must account to Cabinet and to the Parliament for ensuring that the departments for which they are responsible carry out their functions properly and effectively. The Constitution binds the Parliament, the Cabinet, Ministers, and the Public Service as core entities within the State's public administrative system.

Therefore, Good Government requires a professional public service, efficiently managed, with well-defined accountability arrangements. The Permanent Secretary as the administrative head of the ministry or department of government has constitutional and statutory responsibilities for the efficient operations of the Ministry or Department. The Permanent Secretary anchors the department in the laws and regulations governing the Public Service; ensuring that the Minister is informed and kept abreast of the implementation of projects and programs, and other developments within the Ministry;

providing objective, evidence-based advice, and implementing the decisions of the Government.

As the Accounting Officer for the Ministry, the Permanent Secretary has defined financial responsibilities as follows: 1. Accountable to Parliament for all monies allocated or voted to that department in the annual Estimates of Revenue and Expenditure. 2. Guides and supervises the preparation of the annual estimates and manages the budgetary allocations, ensuring expenditures are in keeping with the budget and statutory requirements. 3. Takes steps to reduce or eliminate waste, undertaking periodic reviews of the operations of the ministry or department ensuring adherence to planned programs, projects, other activities, and legislative requirements.

In the performance of their duties Permanent Secretaries and public officers in general are required to function in an impartial manner; be politically neutral in their work, serving the current Minister and by extension the Government in such a manner that will enable them to serve any future holder of the office or Government.

In conclusion, the Constitution binds the Parliament, the Cabinet, Ministers, and the Public Service as core entities within the State's public administrative system, and they are responsible for maintaining Good Government as enshrined in the Constitution.

Knowledge is power and experience is the greatest teacher.

# State of Government Finances

## Government Finances and the Economy as of 31st March 2022

Fiscal policy, which is the main instrument of economic management, is implemented through the execution of the annual national budget; and hence the importance of monitoring its implementation. To facilitate the monitoring of the National Budget, the Government publishes monthly data on the fiscal performance on the Ministry of Finance website www.finance.gd/index.php/fiscal-reports; and the monthly fiscal summary reports for January to March 2022 have been published.

The review of the Government's finances, based on the monthly fiscal reports, showed that the fiscal performance for the first three months of 2022 was favourable. The budget outturn was better than what the Government targeted to achieve. This was influenced by higher revenue and grants associated with the 'one off receipt in the form of dividends' of $17.5M in January, the receipt of budgetary support in grants of $81M in March, and the increases in tax revenue during the quarter; combined with less than targeted current expenditure. Therefore, the outturn on the current or operational account was stronger than projected, and capital expenditure was higher than the planned spending. Specifically, Government recorded (i) a current account surplus, before budgetary support in 'grants', of $74.1M; (ii) a current account surplus, after budgetary support in 'grants', of $155.1M; (iii) a primary surplus, after 'grants', of $117.9M; (iv) an overall deficit, before 'grants', of $3.9 M; and (v) an overall surplus, after 'grants', of $109.1M.

On the current account, current or operational revenue of $224.8M in the first quarter of 2022 was 19.4 percent or $36.5M more than the $188.3M government projected to collect for that period. The components of revenue that contributed to the higher outturn compared with the targeted amount were not provided in the report. However, with the 'one off receipt in the form of dividends' of $17.5M, non-tax sources of revenue were higher than targeted. Dividends are the receipts from the distribution of profits to shareholders in companies, so this implies that the Government received such funds from its ownership of shares in a company which was not disclosed in the report. The Government received budgetary support, in the form of grants, of $81M, which boosted the financial resources available to the Government during the first quarter.

In comparing developments in 2022 with 2021, the revenue performance for the first quarter of 2022 was stronger than the first quarter of 2021. The current revenue of $224.8M collected in the first quarter of 2022 was $47.2M or 26.6 percent more than that collected in the first quarter of 2021, due to higher revenue from both tax and non-tax sources. The growth in tax revenue was more pronounced for the expenditure related taxes, that is, taxes on goods and services and taxes on international trade. This was influenced by the higher value of the tax base due to the impact of inflation, and an expansion in economic activity during the first quarter. Although there were some constraints on activities during the quarter as a result of the Omicron virus, these were less restrictive and the economic and social impacts were less severe than in the first quarter of 2021. Also, in the first quarter of 2022, increased economic activity was fueled by higher Government capital spending. With the 'one off receipt in the form of dividends', non-tax revenue was significantly higher in the first quarter of 2022, and the receipt of budgetary support strengthened the Government's fiscal position.

Current expenditure was contained below the amount the Government planned to spend during the first quarter. The current or operational expenditure of $150.7M for the first quarter of 2022, was $10.1M or 6.3 percent less than the Government planned spending of $160.8M for that quarter. Except for a marginal increase in transfers and subsidies, all the other components of current expenditure that is, employee compensation, expenditure on goods and services and interest payment, were less than the amount the Government planned to spend during the quarter. When compared with 2021, current or operational expenditure in the first quarter of 2022 was $1.4M more than the expenditure of $149.3M incurred in the first quarter of 2021.

With these developments, the Government realized the current account surplus of $74.1M (before budgetary support) and $155.1M (after budgetary support) for the first quarter of 2022. This surplus was higher than the $27.5M that the Government planned to achieve for the quarter. It was also higher than the current account surplus of $28.3M achieved in 2021.

On the capital account, capital expenditure of $78M, during the first quarter of 2022, was higher than the planned expenditure of $65.2M. The surplus on the current account contributed to the financing of the capital expenditure as capital 'grants' and loans, which together were $34.2M, could not finance the total capital spending. The 'grants' financing was $32M, which was less than the $34.3M in capital 'grants' that the Government planned to spend; and the government received loan financing of $2.2M. The capital spending of $78M in the first quarter of 2022 was higher than the $35.3M spent in the same period in 2021. At the end of the first quarter, capital expenditure was 23.4 percent of the budgeted $333.8M. If this rate of spending is sustained throughout the year, the government would spend the budgeted amount for capital expenditure of $333.8M.

With the favourable developments on the current account, with a current account surplus of $74.1M before budgetary support and \$105M after budgetary support, the fiscal performance in the first quarter of 2022 was better than targeted. The government achieved an overall deficit, before 'grants', of \$3.9M and an overall surplus, after 'grants', of \$109.1M for the first quarter of 2022. In contrast, the Government targeted an overall deficit, before grants, of \$37.7M and an overall deficit, after grants, of \$3.4M. The following table is a summary of the Government's finances for the first quarter of 2022 as derived from the monthly Fiscal Reports:

## Table 1: Central Government Finances in EC\$M

| Government Finances | Targeted 2022 | Actual 2022 | Actual 2021 |
|---|---|---|---|
| Total Revenue and Grants | 222.6 | 337.8 | 212.4 |
| Total Grants | 34.3 | 113 | 34.8 |
| Capital Grants | 34.3 | 32 | 34.8 |
| Current Grants | | 81 | |
| Current Revenue | 188.3 | 224.8 | 177.6 |
| Total Expenditure | 226 | 228.7 | 184.8 |
| Current Expenditure | 160.8 | 150.7 | 149.3 |
| Capital Expenditure | 65.2 | 78 | 35.3 |
| Current Account Balance (Before Grants) | 27.5 | 74.1 | 28.3 |
| Current Account Balance (After Grants) | 27.5 | 155.1 | 28.3 |
| Primary Balance (After Grants) | 6.7 | 117.9 | 35.7 |
| Overall Balance (After Grants) | -3.4 | 109.1 | 27.6 |

Source: Derived from the monthly fiscal reports of the Ministry of Finance for January, February, and March 2022.

The financial resources must be carefully managed. The Court ruling on the payment of pension and gratuity to public officers would increase Government obligations, requiring additional financial resources. With the increased public obligations, fiscal transparency becomes more critical.

The presentation of the financing component of the fiscal account in the Estimates of Revenue and Expenditure for 2022 was a good start to improving fiscal transparency. However, its omission from the reports on actual fiscal performance makes its inclusion in the budget null and void. The inclusion of the financing component of the fiscal account in the published fiscal reports, and the operational account of the National Transformation Fund would allow for a more comprehensive analysis of the government finances.

The following relating to fiscal transparency, which was reported in previous articles, still needs to be addressed:

"However, there is a fundamental deviation from the standard practice for fiscal reports. Each monthly report needs to include a summary of the year-to-date financial position of the government as at the date of the published report. Currently, to assess the state of the government finances over a period, the data in each of the individually published monthly fiscal reports must be aggregated. This practice inhibits persons who do not have the time, energy, and technical knowledge to consolidate the monthly reports from assessing the state of the government finances."

In summary, the Government finances were favourable during the first quarter of 2022. This was due to higher revenue associated with 'one off receipt in the form of dividends', budgetary support, and a general increase in tax revenue; combined with less than targeted current expenditure. Prudent financial management is critical as the Court ruling on pension and gratuity has increased the public debt and the cost of Government current operations. The scrutiny of the public finances would become even more critical. The systems for fiscal management and providing information to the public should be implemented including the submission of the annual report of the Director of

Audit to Parliament in accordance with Section 82 of the Constitution, and sections 66 and 67 of the Public Finance Management Act (2015).

Knowledge is power and experience is the greatest teacher.

## Government Finances and the Economy as of 30th June 2022

An assessment of the state of the public finances is important at this junction, as the new administration of the National Democratic Congress (NDC) assumes responsibility for managing the economy. The following assessment of the public finances as of June 2022 is based solely on the aggregation of the monthly fiscal reports for the months of January to June that were published on the Ministry of Finance website www.finance.gd/index.php/fiscal-reports.

There are some deficiencies in using the published monthly fiscal reports for undertaking a comprehensive assessment of the public finances. Specifically, the published fiscal reports do not include the financing of Government operations and the status of the National Transformation Fund. These deficiencies which result in a lack of fiscal transparency and accountability are outlined in the articles 'Government Finances and the Economy' in the published book 'Budget Alert: Fiscal Policy Issues in Grenada in 2021'. However, as an urgent action, each monthly fiscal report needs to include a summary of the year-to-date financial position of the Government as at the date of the published report. This should not be prolonged as in this era of Information and Communication Technology (ICT), it could be easily accomplished.

The review showed that the fiscal performance for the first six months of 2022 was favourable, as the budget outturn was better than what the Government targeted to achieve. This was due primarily to higher revenue and grants, as total expenditure, particularly capital spending, was higher than targeted. Specifically, for the first six months Government recorded (i) a current account surplus, before budgetary support in 'grants', of $118.1M; (ii) a current account surplus, after budgetary support in 'grants', of $199.1M; (iii) a primary surplus, after 'grants', of $123.9M; (iv) an overall deficit, before 'grants', of $51.7M; and (v) an overall surplus, after 'grants', of $99.3M.

On the current account, current or operational revenue of $427.7M in the first six months of 2022 was 17.9 percent or $64.8 M more than the $362.9M government projected to collect for that period. The components of revenue that contributed to the higher outturn compared with the targeted amount were not provided in the 'Fiscal Summary Report'. However, the inflationary effects on tax revenue would have contributed to the higher than projected revenue. Also, with the 'one off receipt in the form of dividends' of $17.5M in January, non-tax sources of revenue were higher than targeted. The Government received budgetary support, in the form of grants, of $81M in March which boosted the financial resources available to the Government.

While current revenue outpaced the amount the Government planned to collect, current expenditure was contained below the amount the Government planned to spend for the first six months. Current or operational expenditure of $309.6M for the first six months of 2022, was $18.9M or 5.8 percent less than the Government planned spending of $328.5M for that period. Except for a marginal increase in transfers and subsidies, all the other components of current expenditure that is, employee compensation, expenditure on goods and services and interest payment, were less than the amount the Government planned to spend during the first six months of 2022. With these developments, the Government realized the current account surplus of $118.1M (before budgetary support) and $199.1M (after budgetary support) for the first six months of 2022. This surplus was higher than the $34.4M that the Government planned to achieve for the first six months of 2022.

The outturn from Government current operations was also stronger in the first six months of 2022 compared with the same period in 2021, due to the higher revenues, combined with lower current expenditure. The current revenue of $427.7M collected in the first half of 2022 was $70.2M or 19.6 percent more than that collected in the first six months of 2021, influenced by higher revenue from both tax and non-tax sources. Revenue from all categories of taxes increased. However, the growth in tax revenue was more pronounced for the expenditure related taxes, that is, taxes on domestic goods and services and taxes on international trade. This was influenced by the higher value of the tax base due to the impact of inflation, and an expansion in economic activity during the first half of the year.

The inflationary period persisted in 2022. The inflation rate from Grenada's main sources of imports increased from 7.5 percent in January to 9.1 percent in June for the USA, and from 5.5 percent to 9.4 percent for the UK and from 5.1 percent to 8.1 percent for Canada for the same period. Higher prices for imported goods would have contributed to higher tax revenue. The growth in economic activity also accounted for the higher revenue. Tourist arrivals, a main driver of economic activity, increased significantly during the first six months, reflecting the opening up of the economy. Also, the construction sector would have expanded, fueled by higher Government capital spending. With the 'one off receipt in the form of dividends', non-tax revenue was significantly higher in the first half of 2022, and the receipt of budgetary support strengthened the Government's fiscal position.

When compared with 2021, current or operational expenditure in the first six months of 2022 was $9.2M less than the expenditure of $318.8M incurred in the first six months of 2021. Except for transfers and subsidies, all the categories of current expenditure were less in 2022 compared with 2021. Consequently, the current account surplus of $118.1M (before budgetary support) and $199.1M (after budgetary support) for the first six months of 2022 was significantly higher than the $38.7M recorded for the first half of 2021.

On the capital account, capital expenditure of $169.8M, during the first half of 2022, was higher than the planned expenditure of $132.8M, and the $86.4M spent in the same period in 2021. The significant deviation between planned spending and actual spending occurred in the months of March, May, and June. The report did not provide information on the projects that were accelerated during this period, but this could be linked to the surge in spending prior to the general elections.

While capital expenditure was higher than planned, the 'grants' spending of $70M was in line with the targeted $69.9M that the Government planned to spend. At the end of the first six months, capital expenditure was 50.9 percent of the budgeted $333.8M. If this rate of spending is sustained throughout the year, the government would spend the budgeted amount for capital expenditure of $333.8M.

With the favourable developments on the current account, the fiscal performance in the first six months of 2022 was better than targeted. The government achieved an overall deficit, before 'grants', of $51.7M and an overall surplus, after 'grants', of $99.3M for the first six months of 2022. In contrast, the Government targeted an overall deficit, before grants, of $98.4M and an overall deficit, after grants, of $28.5M. The table below is a summary of the Government's finances for the first six months of 2022 as derived from the monthly fiscal reports for January to June.

This is a partial analysis, and a comprehensive report on the public finances for the first six months of 2022 should be available at the time of the submission of the Mid-Year Fiscal Policy Report to Parliament in keeping with Subsection 25 of the Public Finance Management Act (2015). The actual state of the public finances for 2021 should be available on the submission of the annual report of the Director of Audit to Parliament in accordance with Section 82 of the Constitution, and Sections 66 and 67 of the Public Finance Management Act (2015).

## Table 1: Central Government Finances EC$M

| Government Finances | Targeted 2022 | Actual 2022 | Actual 2021 |
|---|---|---|---|
| Total Revenue and Grants | 432.8 | 578.7 | 429.1 |
| Total Grants | 69.9 | 151 | 71.6 |
| Capital Grants | 69.9 | 70 | 71.6 |
| Current Grants | 0 | 81 | 0 |
| Current Revenue | 362.9 | 427.7 | 357.5 |
| Total Expenditure | 461.3 | 479.4 | 405.2 |
| Current Expenditure | 328.5 | 309.6 | 318.8 |
| Capital Expenditure | 132.8 | 169.8 | 86.4 |
| Current Account Balance (Before Current Grants) | 34.4 | 118.1 | 38.7 |
| Current Account Balance (After Current Grants) | 34.4 | 199.1 | 38.7 |
| Primary Balance (After Grants) | 0.2 | 123.9 | 49.1 |
| Overall Balance (After Grants) | -28.5 | 99.3 | 23.7 |

Source: Derived from the monthly fiscal reports of the Ministry of Finance for the first six months of 2022.

Knowledge is power and experience is the greatest teacher.

## A Mix of Direct and Indirect Taxes

Traditionally, taxes have been the main source of government operational revenue in the countries of the Eastern Caribbean Currency Union (ECCU). This high dependence on tax revenue began to change in the 1980s as some countries increased their dependence on inflows from the Citizenship by Investment (CBI) programme. In Grenada, the Citizenship by Investment Act came into effect in 2013 and inflows from the CBI programme contributed to Government non-tax current revenue and to capital revenue which is classified by the Government as 'grants'. The CBI as a source of revenue is expected to be volatile. Therefore, taxes would remain an integral part of Government revenue, particularly to finance current operations.

The burden of taxation would continue to be debated as taxes are compulsory payments and are not directly linked to the receipt of a particular good or service. Government uses the tax revenue collected to provide public goods and services for the benefit of the population. This leads to the issue of who should bear the cost of providing these public goods and services, and how this cost should be shared among the population, referred to as the fairness of the tax system. The fairness or equity of taxation is associated with the payment of taxes based on the ability to pay, that is, persons with higher income should pay a greater proportion of their income in taxes or bear a greater burden of the cost of government.

To facilitate analysis of the fairness of the tax system, taxes are classified into two types: direct and indirect taxes. The direct taxes are levied on individuals or entities, and they are generally tailored to the economic circumstances of the individual or entity. The tax is expected to be borne by the individual or entity on whom it is levied, and it cannot be shifted to another individual or entity. In Grenada, the main direct taxes are the personal income tax, corporate tax, withholding tax and property tax. Indirect taxes are levied on transactions in the economy. While indirect taxes are paid by an individual or entity, based on the legislation, the tax is passed on and therefore paid by the consumers and clients. These are mainly the Value Added Tax (VAT), import duty, customs service charge and petrol tax.

It is necessary to maintain a balance of direct and indirect taxes. The tax system should not be so heavily dependent on direct taxes of income and profits that it impedes investment and production. At the same time, too much dependence on indirect taxes places a greater burden on the no and low-income segments of the population.

There is no scientific method for determining the balance between direct and indirect taxes in a country. It is dependent on the philosophy of the government, the nature of the economy and the existing social and economic conditions, particularly related to the distribution of income and the level of poverty. However, countries with high income generating resources generally have a high intake of revenue from taxes on income and profits. This is the case in the petroleum base economy of Trinidad and Tobago where direct taxes accounted for 68.2 percent of tax revenue in 2019. A comparison of countries with similar characteristics provides a guide to assessing the mix of direct and indirect taxes. In Barbados, with a per capita income of EC$46,000, direct taxes accounted for 33 percent of tax revenue in 2019. The countries of the ECCU, although fundamentally similar, there are some slight variations, influencing the combination of direct and indirect taxes. Among the independent countries of the ECCU, there are the tourism dependent countries of Antigua and Barbuda and St Kitts and Nevis with high per capita income of EC$40,540 and of EC$44,123 respectively, comparable with Barbados. These countries have maintained a philosophy of no comprehensive taxation on personal income which has determined the mix of direct and indirect taxes.

In Antigua and Barbuda, there is an education levy which is equivalent to the taxation of personal income. Consequently, direct taxes accounted for 16 percent of tax revenue and indirect taxes accounted for 84 percent of tax revenue in 2019. In St Kitts and Nevis, where the full-fledged personal income tax was abolished, the structure of the taxes on income and profits differs from Antigua and Barbuda. The personal income tax is in the form of a social services levy that is paid in equal percentages by the employers and the employees, and along with the corporate income tax there is a business levy. With this structure, direct taxes accounted for 32.7 percent of tax revenue and indirect taxes accounted for 67.3 percent of tax revenue in 2019. For the tax system in Antigua and Barbuda, the low-income groups pay a higher proportion of their income in taxes, compared with the system in Barbados and St Kitts and Nevis.

The other independent countries namely, Dominica, Grenada, Saint Lucia and St Vincent and the Grenadines have greater similarities. They are more agricultural based and are developing tourism and financial services. The per capita income is comparatively lower, estimated at EC$20,463 in Dominica, EC$26,893 in Grenada, EC$30,877 in Saint Lucia and EC$20,189 in St Vincent and the Grenadines. They exhibit some similar social indicators such as high youth unemployment as reported in Saint Lucia (35.95%), and St Vincent and the Grenadines (39.76%) in 2019 and in Grenada (38.6%) in

2021; and high poverty rates of 20.3 percent in Saint Lucia (2016) and 25 percent in Grenada (2019).

Among these countries, the ratio of direct and indirect taxes to tax revenue was 20 percent direct taxes and 80 percent indirect taxes in Dominica, 25.9 percent direct and 74.1 percent indirect in Grenada, 26.6 percent direct and 73.4 percent indirect in Saint Lucia and 32.6 percent direct and 67.4 percent indirect in St Vincent and the Grenadines. Except for Antigua and Barbuda with the philosophy of no personal income tax, and Dominica which is dominated by agriculture production, Grenada's tax structure is more dependent on indirect taxes compared with the neighbouring countries, implying that for the tax system in Grenada, the lower income earners pay a higher portion of their income in taxes. In the aftermath of the Covid-19 Pandemic, there was a notable shift in the dependence on indirect taxes in Grenada and the ratio moved to 23 percent direct taxes and 77 percent indirect taxes in 2021. This implies that the no and low-income segment of the population were paying an increasing portion of their income in taxes. Among the other countries of the ECCU, this increased dependence on indirect taxes was also a feature of Dominica's tax system.

The increased post Pandemic burden of taxes on the lower income group could be alleviated by improved targeting of zero-rated goods and services, particularly frequently purchased goods and services that emerged with the onset of the Covid-19 Pandemic. The application of the customs service charge should be examined. The customs service charge was introduced as an administrative cost recovery. It was expected to be maintained at a relatively low rate, and a maximum of 5 percent was considered appropriate. The customs service charge is integrated in the tax system and is applied on a compounded base of the CIF value of the good and the import duty. Then the VAT is further levied on the compounded base of the CIF value of the good, the import duty, and the customs service charge. The customs service charge should be eliminated from the compounded calculation of the taxes of imported goods; and it should stand as a separate charge that is levied on the CIF value of the goods.

The mix of direct and indirect taxes is based on the philosophy of the government and the state of the economy. In countries with high unemployment and poverty, high dependence on indirect taxes places a great burden on the no and low-income segments of the population.

Knowledge is power and experience is the greatest teacher.

## Financing Government Operations

The Financing, which is the most important component of the fiscal account, is often omitted from the presentation of government finances. Government operations could result in an overall surplus, that is, total domestic revenue and grants or monetary gifts are more than Government total expenditure. Alternatively, Government operations could result in a deficit, that is, total expenditure is more than total domestic revenue and grants or monetary gifts.

The financing component of the fiscal account shows how the Government utilizes a surplus or how a deficit is financed. At the end of June 2022, the Government realized an overall surplus after grants of $99.3M as outlined in a previous article on 'Government Finances and the Economy'. If the financing component was included in the accounts, it would have provided information on how that surplus was utilized.

The financing component of the accounts is important in this environment where the report of the Director of Audit has not been submitted to Parliament as prescribed by the Constitution. Therefore, the financing could be used as a 'rapid test' to check the integrity of the fiscal account. In countries with limited fiscal data, and where information is available on government transactions with financial institutions and creditors, the financing component is used to determine the outcome of government operations.

The construction of the financing component of the fiscal account requires the application of knowledge with accuracy and precision. This process could be compared with a medical doctor undertaking heart or brain surgery. The operation is delicate and requires accuracy and precision, as an error could affect the functioning of the body. Similarly, errors in calculating the financing could affect the integrity of the fiscal accounts.

The calculated financing must be equivalent to the overall surplus or the overall deficit. In the case of the overall surplus after grants of $99.3M at the end of June 2022, the total financing should account for this surplus. The financing is determined by an aggregation of government transactions during the year, that is, loans and deposits with domestic financial institutions, external financial institutions and creditors, and any other entities with whom the Government engages in financial transactions.

Consistent with international standards, loan disbursement is not classified as receipts and principal debt repayment is not included in expenditure in undertaking analysis of government operations. These are classified as financing and hence the importance of including the financing component in the fiscal accounts. The financing shows the impact of government operations on the Central Government debt and by extension the stock of public sector debt.

The financing of government operations from domestic sources is generally reflected in its net transactions (borrowing and depositing) with the Eastern Caribbean Central Bank, the National Insurance Scheme, financial institutions mainly the commercial banks and credit unions, and any benefactor willing to engage in financial transactions with the government. An examination of the accounts of these financial institutions would determine whether the Government deposited funds with or borrowed from the institutions and entities. The aggregation of these financial transactions provides information on the impact of Government operations on the Central Government domestic debt. If the aggregated loaned funds from the domestic institutions exceed deposits, the Central Government domestic debt has increased. Alternatively, if deposits exceed the loaned funds, Central Government domestic debt has declined.

Financing from external sources is related to Government transactions with external financial institutions and creditors. The external financing shows how much external loan funds were disbursed to the Government by creditors and how much was government principal debt repayment to external creditors.   The net effect of disbursement and principal repayment provides information on the impact of government operations on the external debt. If disbursements exceed principal repayment, the Central Government external debt has increased. However, if principal repayment exceeds disbursement, Central Government external debt has declined. The Government may hold external assets and during the fiscal year either increased or reduced its stock of external assets. This is recorded in the financing as changes in foreign assets. The transactions do not impact on the public debt.

The accumulation of arrears is a peculiar form of financing government operations. It could be described as 'forced borrowing' from suppliers as the government has received goods and services but no payment has been made to the suppliers. It is effectively an interest free loan to the Government from suppliers of goods and services. The Government could either accumulate arrears which is the forced borrowing, or it could reduce its arrears with its creditors.

The financing component provides important information on whether government operations resulted in an increase or decrease in the public debt. Therefore, there are checks and balances to ensure that the financing is correctly constructed. The reported financing should be consistent with the detailed information provided in Vote 22, 'charges on account of the public debt', in the Estimates of Revenue and Expenditure and the Annual Borrowing Plan that is included in the Medium-term Debt Strategy. The financing items must also be consistent with the other economic accounts, specifically the financial sector and the balance of payment. The Government records of its loans and deposit transactions with financial institutions should be consistent with that reported by the institutions. The official external transactions in the form of loan disbursement and principal debt repayment must be consistent with that reported in the balance of payment. The changes in the Government's foreign assets must also be registered in the balance of payment.

Given the importance of the financing, it is desirable that the actual financing for 2021, the preliminary financing for 2022, and the planned financing for 2023, be included in the Estimates of Revenue and Expenditure for 2023. Additionally, the public accounts for 2021 could only be properly closed after the Report of the Director of Audit is presented to Parliament. This step in the budgetary process has remained outstanding over the previous years and needs to be addressed to improve fiscal transparency and accountability.

Knowledge is power and experience is the greatest teacher.

# In Pursuit of Transforming
# The Economy

## Budget Time Again

The public would be eagerly awaiting the presentation of the national budget for 2023. The transformative agenda of the National Democratic Congress (NDC) administration, for at least the next three years, should then be outlined. Within this three-years framework, the public would be informed of the policies, programs, and projects for 2023, the expenditure associated with these, and the sources of financing for the expenditures. These would be documented in the Parliamentary Approved Estimates of Revenue and Expenditure for 2023.

The policies, programmes and projects should aim at transforming the economy to "A Sustainable, Equitable and Prosperous Grenada for All". The information presented in the 2023 national budget should be steps to achieving this vision. The current economic and social conditions in the country should form the basis for constructing the building blocks to the transformed economy. Therefore, the assessment of the economy that accompanies the national budget should focus on the indicators that need to be changed to signal the movement to a transformed economy.

While the economic assessment would include the usual trends in the macro-economic variables and developments in the economic, financial, fiscal, and external sectors, there should be an emphasis on the challenges in the economy and some of the structural issues that need to be addressed. These include i. the trend in agriculture production; ii. the performance of agriculture exports; iii. the trend in the food import bill; iv. the state of agro-processing and agri-business; v. developments in the fishing industry and other marine resources; vi. the status of the creative industries; vii. the foreign exchange outflows to external agents for the importation of services; and viii. the efficiency of doing business in Grenada.

The social sectors should be given equal importance in the assessment of the economy. The areas of focus should include developments in education, health and other social services, and the dynamics of deviant behaviour, unemployment, and poverty. A refocusing of the assessment of the economy to highlight the challenges and the structural imbalances would be consistent with pursuing a transformative agenda.

The preparation, approval, implementation, and evaluation of the budget are anchored in the legislative framework. The budget process is guided by the Constitution, and the accompanying legislations are the Public Finance Management Act, the Debt Management Act, the Fiscal Responsibility Act, and the Audit Act. The existence of this legislative framework did not prevent the occurrence of financial dilemmas and fiscal mysteries. Also, numerous recommendations have been put forward for the reform of the Fiscal Responsibility Act. The issue is whether there is a need for legislative reforms, or whether the system for 'Good Government' requires an overhaul, or a combination of legislative and administrative reforms. The Parliament is established for the 'Good Government' of the country, and this should be foremost in transforming the economy.

The contents of the national budget for 2023, which would be presented in the budget speech and the Estimates of Revenue and Expenditure, should show signs of implementing a transformative agenda with the ultimate goal of eradicating poverty. The transformation of the economy would be an ongoing process and would, at times, be hindered by unforeseen circumstances. However, it is important to establish targets to be achieved on the path to transforming the economy. The Government has identified some critical areas in the transformative agenda, and the 2023 national budget should include policies, programmes, and projects that signal that the country is moving in that direction. A feature of the 2023 national budget would therefore be which of the components of the transformation agenda would be developed into policies, programmes, and projects for 2023.

The projected economic growth rate for 2023 and the following two years would be of significance. Foremost among the outcomes of the transformation agenda is achieving sustainable economic growth while i. diversifying the economy; ii. strengthening linkages among the sectors in the economy; iii. improving food and nutrition security; and iv. creating employment, particularly among the youths.

The initiatives for transforming the economy, as outlined in the NDC Manifesto and the Throne speech of 31st August 2022, are expected to be integrated in the Medium-term Economic and Social Development Strategy and the accompanying Public Sector Investment Programme. While these policies and programme documents are being prepared, there are major policies that could be identified, some of which would need to be included in the 2023 national budget.

Fundamental to transforming the economy is the proposal for reforming and developing the productive sectors which include, among other proposals:

i.  The development and integration of agriculture, fisheries and marine resources, tourism, creative industries, culture, and ICT while protecting the environment.

ii.     Improving the value-added in the economy by developing agri-business, fish processing and cannabis industries in medical and hemp products.

iii.     Re-invigorating the spice industry by encouraging farmers to engage in large scale replanting of local spices.

iv.     Reforming the Marketing and National Importing Board; and integrating the Grenada Cocoa Association and the Grenada Cooperative Nutmeg Association.

Therefore, in the 2023 national budget, elements of these policies and programmes should be included in the Vote for the Ministry of Economic Development, Planning, Tourism and ICT, Creative Economy, Agriculture and Lands, Fisheries and Cooperatives. As a stimulus to the reform process, a feature of the budget should be an incentive package for entrepreneurs, particularly for supporting the emerging activities in agri-business, fishing and marine resources, the cannabis industries, the creative industries, and digital based businesses.

Improved economic infrastructure is required to support the transformative agenda. This has implications for telecommunication and internet network, public utilities of water and electricity, the road network, and seaport and airport facilities. The proposals in the budget should reflect the unique circumstances of a tri-island state and the infrastructural needs for connectivity, and the development of the marine resources in Carriacou and Petit Martinique. While some of these areas are not directly under the control of Central Government, the Government should be influential in the developments in these areas through its participation in public enterprises.

The efficient delivery of social services is critical to the development of the transformed economy. Therefore, the proposals from the Ministries of Health, Education, and Social Development should feature prominently in the Medium-term

Economic and Social Development Strategy, and elements should be included in the 2023 national budget. In health, the main proposals are for the construction of a modern hospital with teaching facilities, introduction of national health insurance, provision of health services in communities, and support for the training of personnel for the delivery of health services. The main proposals in education include the provision of free education up to the tertiary level; reforming the school curriculum to incorporate training in areas that would support transformative industries, the digital economy, sports, and culture; providing vocational education; and strengthening community facilities to make education accessible to the population. The policy decision has been taken to provide free education up to the secondary school level. This would need to be extended to the tertiary level.

The budget should include proposals to address the plight of the no-income and low-income segments of the population. Therefore, there should be policies for influencing the distribution of income through the rationalization of the social safety net programme, proposals for the review of the minimum wage, and the modification of the tax system to ensure that it is not over burdensome on the population. Major planks for people empowerment and wealth creation are the proposals for increasing the housing stock and regularizing the land titles for holders of government lands.

Elements of the policies, programmes, and projects for transforming the economy must be identifiable in the 2023 national budget. The Medium-term Economic and Social Development Strategy should incorporate most of the proposals for transforming the economy, and these should be manifested in the Public Sector Investment Programme. Appropriate targets and benchmarks should be included in the Medium-term Economic and Social Development

Strategy to facilitate the monitoring and evaluation of the transformation of the economy.

Knowledge is power and experience is the greatest teacher.

## Transformational Development and the Transformation Mindset – Part 1

In this article, the perspectives of Economist Dr. Roxanne Brizan – St. Martin on the idea of transformative development is presented. The Government has indicated that it is embarking on a transformational agenda and that all citizens and institutions should be part of the process. Dr. Brizan-St. Martin was invited to address senior managers and other members of staff of the Ministry of Agriculture and Lands, Forestry, Fisheries and Cooperatives at their retreat which was held under the theme "Transformative Development: Ensuring Food Security and Sustainable Agricultural Development."

This Part 1 article contextualizes the issue of transformative development whilst Part 2 addresses issues of transformational leadership and the transformation mindset.

In contextualizing the issues of food and nutrition security and sustainable agricultural development, it is important to remember our context as a small island developing state; one in which we are faced with many structural vulnerabilities and other challenges including challenges with fiscal space and the need to be efficient in our resource use. As such, each department or division under the Ministry has a responsibility in this agenda of agricultural development, improving food and nutrition security.

When we speak of *sustainable* agricultural development, we are taking it to the realm of generational viability. Therefore, the systems, processes, and plans developed to ensure agricultural development and food and nutrition security should be one in which future generations can benefit. With sustainable agriculture and food and nutrition security, a country's populace can have more meaningful, happier lives where there is hope for better lives for future generations. This can be achieved by ensuring an enabling environment for good governance, reducing the spread of diseases, boosting self-reliance and less dependence on foreign products-just to name a few.

To reiterate, the definition of sustainable development is "development that meets the needs of the present, without compromising the ability of future generations to meet their own needs."

This concept of transformational development is defined:

i.    In Sociology, as the process through which children, families and communities identify and overcome the obstacles that prevent them from living life in all its fullness.

ii.    In the spiritual sense, it speaks to holistic care – meeting community needs holistically. In this spiritual context, of interest is a blog Wycliffe Bible Translators, detailing the five main principles of transformational development:

    a)    Community empowerment and participatory involvement. This means that an outsider should not do for the community what they can do for themselves.

    b)    Transformational development is not top down. The community is the one that sets the agenda and identifies the priorities.

    c)    Practitioners follow an asset-based approach. Before trying to fix problems, identify and focus on what is already working well.

d) It is important that both the community and the development organisation bring value to the project. Community and development organisations should be equal partners, both bringing something valuable to the table.

e) Communities speak into what needs to be changed and the effectiveness of change. Mindsets!!! Mindsets!!!!! Mindsets!!!!!

When we combine these principles, we get some sense of what transformative development entails: community, participation, empowerment, self-reliance, resilience, mindset, evaluation, and re-evaluation.

The task before you as you plan and pave the way forward for the Ministry, is a transformational project – one that is substantive in its impact. It will take you through a metamorphosis that changes, on a fundamental level, the way you function on a day-to-day basis. This requires transformational leadership and a transformational mindset.

As senior managers within the Ministry, displaying transformational leadership is critical to the agenda and the achievement of transformational development. What you are striving for is cultural change – encouraging and inspiring each other and by extension the nation to innovate and create change that will be for the benefit of all.

The next article addresses the concept of transformational leadership and the transformation mindset.

Knowledge is power and experience is the greatest teacher.

## Transformational Development and the
## Transformation Mindset – Part 2

In Part 1 of this article, Economist Dr. Roxanne Brizan – St. Martin contextualized the notion of transformative development. In this Part 2 article, Dr. Roxanne Brizan – St. Martin presents on transformational leadership and the transformation mindset.

The concept of transformational leadership is not a new concept. It was introduced in 1978 by James MacGregor Burns in his research on political leaders. In this research, he defined Transformational Development as a process in which "leaders and followers help each other to advance to a higher level of morale and motivation." He further highlighted the difference between transformational and transactional leadership in which the latter does not strive for cultural change in the organisation but rather works with the existing culture whereas the transformational leaders can try to change organisational culture.

What senior managers are striving for is cultural change – encouraging and inspiring each other and by extension the nation to innovate and create change that will be for the benefit of all.

In the execution of this transformational leadership, it is important that managers are:

1) Good listeners – recognizing that you may not always have the answers (this requires a lot of humility). It will help you understand your teammates and open the door to productive collaboration.

2) Adaptable and innovative – you need to be cognizant of changes – recognize it, acknowledge it in all its elements and capacities but also make rapid adjustments without compromising your strategic goals.

3) Inspiring – when employees are inspired there is better performance and effort. This requires creating a sense of purpose for your teams – creating an environment where everyone understands, values, and appreciates their vital role in the process.

4) Accountable – key to good governance – this sets an example for junior members of staff to also accept accountability in their work. This provides a foundation of communication, trust, and consistent engagement. Accountability means taking responsibility for your own actions, behaviours, performances, and decisions. Everyone has a part to play in this regard. Lack of accountability damages the team and should not be a core part of the culture of the organisation and team. Systems to ensure accountability can include:

   - Leading by example.
   - Setting individual and team goals.
   - Working on feedback skills...key here is two-way feedback.
   - Keep track of commitments and hold each other accountable.

5) Have integrity – being honest, ethical, and worthy of trust. It involves honouring commitments, keeping promises, and being credible.

These can be summarized into what James Burns calls individualized consideration, intellectual stimulation, inspirational motivation, and idealized influence.

With these qualities, you will be able to garner not just the commitment from other members of staff/colleagues but the mindset that is needed to effect overall organisational change. Therefore, a transformation mindset matters.

A transformational leader must have this mindset in order to effect personal change or change in others. If mindsets are not properly aligned, then reshaping the culture of the organisation is going to be very difficult. We should be reminded that culture is shaped and solidified over time through mindsets and behaviours.

With the advent of the COVID-19 pandemic came the unveiling or further exposure of our vulnerabilities, challenges and even lack of foresight as it relates to issues such as Food Security. However, I revert to the Chinese proverb which states that "Where there is Danger, there is Opportunity." The reliance on the legacy mindset, while important, is not sufficient. A legacy mindset is present when persons are not desirous of changing how they do things, nor are they interested in learning new skills. This mindset is based on knowledge, skills and behaviours that delivered success in the past.

However, transformational mindset embraces and owns changes, requires creativity, and insight – this mindset sets the tone for competitive advantage; knowing when to control and protect and when it's time to create and connect; from being smart to being wise. With this mindset, transformation becomes central to who you are as a ministry and what you do.

While you plan and build as a team, it is important to be conscious of menaces which work against a transformational mindset; overconfidence, being entrenched in orthodoxy, staying within your comfort zones, thinking too short-term, insular thinking and behaviours and lack of strategic clarity. Rather, it requires growth, investing time and effort to change the approach and combining decision-making with evidence. This does not mean blind acceptance or complacency but committing to a growth mindset to continuously find new ideas and perspectives.

Transformation involves a **conscious** and **committed** departure from the current state. This is critical if you are to go beyond what is expected while working on a shared vision. Transformation development, therefore, is hinged on the people process – having a transformational mindset and exhibiting transformational leadership. Remember leadership does not equate to management. Management directs using positional power and is about planning whereas leadership relies on relational power and is about inspiring.

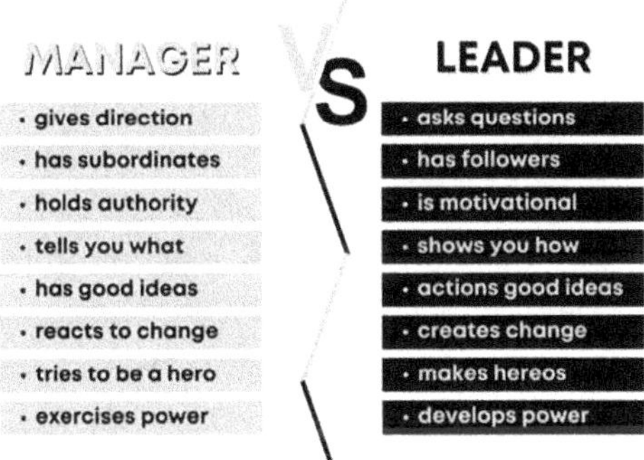


Let us focus on community, partnerships, and evidence-based solutions for sustainability. Displaying transformational leadership is critical to the agenda and the achievement of transformational development. What you are striving for is cultural change – encouraging and inspiring each other and by extension the nation to innovate and create change that will be for the benefit of all.

Knowledge is power and experience is the greatest teacher.

## The 2023 National Budget: An Integrated
## Approach to Development – Part 1

The national budget for 2023 presented an integrated approach to economic development, and, if implemented as planned, could lead to a higher standard of living. An analysis of the 2023 national budget is undertaken in two parts. This Article, Part 1, highlights and assesses the framework and the economic and social context of the budget. The next Article, Part 2, is an assessment of the policy proposals and projected fiscal outcomes of the budget.

The national budget was presented within a defined framework which made it easy to follow logically. It was presented under the theme "Vision 2035: People-Centered Transformation Laying the Foundation for Resilience, Empowerment and Growth". Consistent with good practices in budgeting, the budget was anchored on the five pillars in the National Sustainable Development Plan (NSDP). Under the pillars of the NSDP, the six strategic focus areas were outlined in the budget speech.

This framework was a good approach to the presentation of the budget and encompasses the main areas for policy intervention by the Government. Within the short period after getting into office from 24th June 2022, the Government must be applauded for holding consultations, developing the framework for the budget, and presenting the budget prior to the beginning of the fiscal year. Additionally, the budget speech and the Estimates of Revenue and Expenditure were accompanied with the legally required documents.

The synopsis of economic development in Grenada points to the weak global environment which would undoubtedly have a negative impact on the domestic economy. There are also high downside risks and, if they materialize, would impact the domestic economy, and would need quick policy responses by the Government. However, along with developments in the global economy, domestic developments have a significant impact on the performance of the economy, particularly as capacity exists in the economy. After the steep decline of 13.8 percent in economic activity in 2020, the economy is estimated to have grown by 4.7 percent in 2021 and 6 percent in 2022. Despite the growth in 2021 and 2022, at the end of 2022, economic activity was still below the pre-pandemic level. Therefore, there is existing capacity for economic expansion.

Sustained economic growth is fundamental to transforming the economy and hence the importance of the growth rate. The estimated growth rate of 3.6 percent for 2023 would have taken into consideration the prospects of a weakened global economy, particularly the USA, and the heightened risk in the global economy. However, domestic policies should have a positive impact on economic growth in 2023. In light of government expenditure of $75M in November 2022, and the roll-out of the Covid-19 Economic Stimulus programme which would extend into 2023, and the pronouncements in the 2023 national budget, it is my view that the projected growth rate of 3.6 percent for 2023 could be a very conservative estimate. The estimated growth is placed in the context of the average growth of 7 percent for the Eastern Caribbean Currency Union (ECCU), where countries are registering growth rates as high as 10.4 percent in St. Kitts and Nevis, 8.1 percent in Antigua and Barbuda, 7.6 percent in Anguilla, and 5.9 percent in Saint Lucia. The projected growth rate places Grenada among the slowest growing countries of the ECCU. Alternatively, the issue could be related to the indicators used to compile comparative economic data among the countries in the ECCU which should also be explored.

There are a number of initiatives, when implemented, should stimulate the domestic economy. Among the sectors, the policies to increase flights from major markets, and to facilitate improved inter-island travel; combined with the easing of the administrative requirements for travelling through the airports should contribute to the continued growth in the tourism industry. The policies for increased agricultural production, linking agriculture production to nutrition through the school feeding programme; improving linkages and value added in the economy, particularly, agriculture, agro-processing, the creative industries, and tourism; should result in a more integrated economy. The impact should be manifested in economic growth through increased domestic production and curbing the rate of growth in imports. These initiatives, which are supported by the projects for the development of the social, digital, and economic infrastructure should also contribute to economic growth in 2023. It is in this context that I consider the rate of growth for 2023 to be a conservative estimate.

As the Government pursues the transformation agenda, there should be benchmark data to monitor and report on the process of transformation. Therefore, the assessment of the economy should include benchmark information which would make it align with the transformative agenda. Specifically, the ultimate goal of the Government is to transform the economy to "A Sustainable, Equitable and Prosperous Grenada for All". This implies that there should be details on the existing social conditions in the country, particularly, on unemployment and poverty, and on health and education which are among the priorities for the provision of social services. The data requirements for establishing the benchmarks would be more demanding and would require the gathering of information beyond the existing data gathering systems. However, data gathering and data analysis have been made much easier with the advent of electronic communication systems, and these should be utilized to improve the gathering of information.

Baseline information on the structural variables that must be changing to signal that the economy is transforming should be incorporated prominently in the assessment of the economy. In the productive sectors, the variables that would provide information on the achievement of an improved agriculture sector; diversification and increased linkages in the economy; improved food and nutrition security; and greater use and integration of Information and Communication Technology (ICT) in production and in doing business should be integrated in the assessment of the economy. This would include indicators such as i. The trend in the value of agriculture production in the Gross Domestic Product. This would require overcoming the challenges of collecting comprehensive data on the production of crops, horticulture, livestock, poultry, fishing, and other marine resources. ii. The data on the manufacturing sector would need to be extended beyond the traditional commodities to include developments in agro-processing. The dominance of the cottage type industries could make the collection of data on agro-processing products challenging. However, innovation and technology must be applied in the data gathering process to support the monitoring of the transformation of the economy.  iii. Information systems must be established for incorporating developments in the creative industries, the electronic transacted services, and transactions related to Information and Communication Technology (ICT) in the assessment of economic performance.

These indicators are important as the Government seeks to diversify the economy and to strengthen these sectors for domestic purposes, and to increase exports while curbing the growth in imports. It is therefore important to link the developments in these sectors with the use and earnings of foreign exchange. This would include assessing the food import bill, foreign exchange earnings from the creative industries, cultural and professional services, and the payment to external agencies for such services.

The social sector must be given equal importance. The overall poverty and unemployment rates are generally included in the assessment of the economy. However, the information on unemployment and poverty should be more comprehensive to assess the impact of policy interventions. The gaps in the education system that are being addressed and could be quantified; and the core health indicators that would allow for monitoring and reporting on the transformation process should be integrated in the assessment of the economy.

The focus of the budget on the six priority areas, and the emphasis on the development of linkages which would increase value added in the domestic economy signalled that the Government is seeking to transform the economy. However, transformation of the economy should be measurable by some structural changes. Therefore, the economic and social indicators that would be changing over time should be included in the assessment of the economy.

Knowledge is power and experience is the greatest teacher.

## The 2023 National Budget: An Integrated Approach to Development – Part 2

The focus of the 2023 national budget is on the six priority areas, and the emphasis on the development of linkages which, if successfully implemented, should increase value added in the domestic economy and provide a path to transforming the economy. The transformation of an economy would take time, but the economic and social changes must be evident during the transformation process. The impact of policies, programmes and projects for transforming the economy would depend on effective implementation based on consultation and coordination among Ministries and government entities and with the private sector.

A common feature of Small Island Developing States is the high dependence on the importation of a wide range of goods and services. Grenada is no exception, and similar to the other countries of the Eastern Caribbean Currency Union (ECCU), Grenada imports a variety of goods and services. A component of transforming the economy should be to curb the growth in payments for imported goods and services by utilizing local resources.

The dominance of economic reports on merchandise trade and tourism conceals the payment to external providers for services such as repairs and maintenance services, construction services, financial services, use of intellectual property, and personal, cultural and recreational services. Therefore, education policies to synchronise the school curriculum with the education and skills requirements of the economy, and to develop vocational training should increase the availability of these services locally and curb the growth in the use of foreign exchange for their importation. Increased inflows of foreign exchange from trade in services could also be boosted by the development of the creative and digital economy. These industries not only have the potential for increased exports of culture, recreational and personal services, but for utilizing untapped human resources to reduce unemployment, particularly among the youths.

An integrated economy would be manifested by increased value added through linkages between agriculture and tourism, with the tourism industry also benefiting from the creative and the digital economy and supported by the reforms in the health and education sectors. As part of the strategy for the development of the creative and digital economy, an interim package of tax incentives was granted. The technical committee for reviewing the fiscal incentives would need to work diligently to undertake a comprehensive redesign of the fiscal incentive regime to support the emerging sectors.

Along with the economic policies that could lead to an integrated economy, are the supportive policies for governance and institutional rebuilding, foremost of which are pension and public sector reform. It is hoped that the Pension Committee would bring closure to the issue of pension reform, which has confronted all the countries of the Eastern Caribbean Currency Union. As early as 2005, the Monetary Council of the Eastern Caribbean Central Bank established the Commission on Pension and Pension Administration Reform (Pension Commission) to address the issue of pension and pension reform in the ECCU, and its report was submitted to the Monetary Council. However, the Grenada situation is complicated by the ruling of the Court and the Constitutional provisions, which would inform the work of the Pension Committee.

In the provision of public services, the public sector reform would need to include streamlining the public service to focus on its core functions of providing professional services as envisaged in the Constitution. Much could be done on reforming organisational structures and streamlining procedures and processes, this is necessary but not sufficient for an efficient public service. Public officers must take personal responsibility for being professional, but this must be supported by good management and accountability through a robust performance appraisal system.

Under the pillar for 'Strengthening Regional and International Cooperation', I make a stronger plea for strengthening the OECS Economic Union. There are benefits to be derived as a country and for individuals who do business and interact within the OECS Economic Union. A public awareness programme could contribute to people maximizing the benefits of the Economic Union.

As the country develops agro-processing and the creative and digital economy, the benefits of operating within the wider CARICOM could also be exploited. The scope and avenues for penetrating markets based on CARICOM agreements with the Dominican Republic, Costa Rica, Colombia, Cuba, and Venezuela could be explored.

The policies for addressing the current inflationary period focused on providing targeted relief. The exemption of the sanitary products which is described in economics as inelastic in demand, that is, whatever is the price, the products are needed and must be purchased, should bring some relief to the lower income groups. In this environment, where social and business transactions are undertaken electronically, electricity and internet services are also necessities, and the relief has both social and economic impact. The increase in the tax on alcohol and cigarettes, which serves as a revenue raising measure and a deterrent should be monitored. It could have unintended impacts such as illegal trade, and a reduction in household disposable income as there is increased allocation for the products, accommodated by the reduction in the purchase of other consumer items.

Government finances were stable, with a current account surplus of $308.9M or 8.9 percent of GDP. The comparatively high current account surplus was due to higher non-tax revenue as a result of the reclassification of inflows from the Citizenship by Investment Programme from grants to non-tax revenue in 2023. This reclassification does not affect the overall balance after grants which is an indicator of the impact of government operations on the public debt. The overall surplus after grants is estimated at $62.7M or 1.8 percent of GDP for 2023. The information on the public debt continues to be restricted to the Central Government, and this could be one area for education of the public on the concept of the public debt.

The focus of the budget on increasing linkages and improving value added in the economy should lead to an integrated economy, with the capacity to increase output, exports and employment. The achievement of a well integrated economy with low levels of unemployment and poverty should be the outcome of an integrated approach to development.

Knowledge is power and experience is the greatest teacher.

# Conclusion

The Budget Alert articles for 2022 explore the socio-economic issues of unemployment, poverty, and inflation, indicating that there is the need for disaggregated data to assess the impact of public policy. The articles on the Court decision on the payment of Pension and gratuity to public officers are included for historical purposes.  The state of the government finances is assessed in the context of the implementation of the 2022 national budget. Budget Alert concludes with the expectations and assessment of the national budget for 2023; with a focus on the agenda for transforming the economy.

# Appendix 1: Date of Publication of Articles

## Table 1: Date of Publications

| Name of Article | Date of Publication |
| --- | --- |
| Exploring Unemployment in Grenada | 28th January 2022 |
| Exploring Poverty in Grenada – Part 1 | 11th February, 2022 |
| Exploring Poverty in Grenada – Part 2 | 25th February, 2022 |
| Inflation: Causes and Consequences – Part 1 | 25th March 2022 |
| Inflation: Causes and Consequences – Part 2 | 1st April 2022 |
| Introductory Statement to the Articles on the Financing of the Payment of Pension and Gratuity | 20th July, 2022 |
| Payment of Pension and Gratuity to Public officers | 16th April, 2022 |
| Financing the Payment of Pension and Gratuity – Part 1 | 8th July 2022 |
| Good Government: Core to Transforming the Economy | 5th August, 2022 |
| Government Finances and the Economy as of 31 March 2022 | 12th May, 2022 |
| Government Finances and the Economy as of 30th June 2022 | 19th August, 2022 |
| A Mix of Direct and Indirect Taxes | 9th September 2022 |
| Financing Government Operations | 18th November, 2022 |
| Budget Time Again | 25th November 2022 |
| Transformational Development and the Transformation Mindset – Part 1 | 14th October 2022 |
| Transformational Development and the Transformation Mindset – Part 2 | 21st October 2022 |
| The 2023 National Budget: An Integrated Approach to Development – Part 1 | 13th January 2023 |
| The 2023 National Budget: An Integrated Approach to Development – Part 2 | 3rd February 2023 |

## The Author

### Ms. Laurel Bain

Ms. Laurel Bain was formerly employed as a Senior Director at the Eastern Caribbean Central Bank. She has strong technical and administrative skills which were strengthened as she served for over 25 years in various positions including that of Deputy Director in the Research Department, Senior Director of the Statistics Department, and Adviser and Senior Director in the Governor's Office.

Ms. Bain has undertaken numerous assessments of the economies of the Eastern Caribbean Currency Union (ECCU) and research on fiscal policy and taxation issues in the ECCU. Ms. Bain has worked extensively with international development agencies and regional institutions. She represented the countries of the ECCU at the IMF and the World Bank, and participated in ongoing dialogue with these institutions.

Ms. Bain was engaged in capacity building programmes in CARICOM. She provided training to senior public officers in Dominica, Montserrat, Anguilla, and trainers in these countries along with The Bahamas and the Turks and Caicos Islands. She has been involved in undertaking assessment and developing training programs for parliamentarians, with Guyana as the pilot.

Ms. Bain is the Author of the books: Fiscal Policy: The Economy, and The Tax Structure of the Member Countries of the ECCB.

Ms. Bain holds a Bachelor of Science (BSc) and Master of Science (MSc) degrees in Economics from the University of the West Indies, St Augustine, Trinidad, and Tobago.

## Contributors

The Articles benefited from the knowledge and experiences of Dr Juliet Melville, Dr. Roxanne Brizan-St.Martin, Mrs. Gemma Bain-Thomas, and Ms. Shanise Hutchinson.

### Dr Juliet A Melville

Dr Juliet A Melville is an Independent Consultant and Director of Venture Research (B'dos) Inc. She has over twenty years of experience in international development work with fifteen of these at the Caribbean Development Bank where she served in various capacities including Acting Director of Economics, Chief Economist, and Chief Research Economist. She possesses strong skills in economic analysis, economic planning and policy formulation, and was routinely involved in the monitoring and analysis of socio-economic developments in Caribbean countries and the wider international community, producing regular reports and providing strategic and operational advice. Dr Melville also led and provided technical support on high-level country missions for policy dialogue with officials on programming, projects, policy-based support, macro-economic management, and economic performance, and maintained ongoing policy dialogue with governments.

Dr Melville is knowledgeable and proficient in all aspects of project cycle management including project appraisal, project planning and implementation, monitoring and evaluation, risk management, and procurement. She has assisted countries in designing operations aimed at improved economic governance, public sector modernization, financial sector stability, fiscal consolidation, and debt sustainability as well as poverty and vulnerability reduction.

Dr Melville is an experienced researcher and was instrumental in the establishment of the Social and Economic Research Unit at CDB. She has publications in the area of poverty, social protection, debt, structural adjustment, regional integration, and transport. She is an accomplished trainer, facilitator, and teacher, and has developed and delivered tertiary level training, seminars, workshops, and conferences.

Dr Melville has collaborated extensively with leading regional and international development agencies. Dr Melville was a Lecturer in Economics at the University of the West Indies (UWI) St, Augustine., and holds degrees in BSc. Economics, MSc. Economics and Ph.D. Economics.

### Dr. Roxanne Brizan-St. Martin

Dr. Roxanne Brizan-St. Martin is an Economist with over seventeen (17) years of experience in research, project management, health accounting, and capacity building in over eleven (11) Caribbean countries, in the area of health and socio-economic development. She specializes in health systems management, health financing and healthcare access options and challenges in the Caribbean. She is also trained in Local Capacity Advocacy and Policy Monitoring for Civil Society Organizations (CSOs), Gender Statistics and Gender Equality, Results Based Project Management, and COVID-19 Contact Tracing and Spatial Econometrics. Dr. Brizan-St. Martin is passionate about development that is transdisciplinary, pro-poor and pro-people which is articulated in the sustainomics framework – "making development more sustainable."

## Mrs. Gemma Bain-Thomas

Mrs. Gemma Bain-Thomas is an Independent Contractor. She has considerable experience in public policy and public administration; having served in a senior capacity in various ministries and departments in the Grenada Public Service for thirty (30) years. Among the senior positions held were that of Secretary to Cabinet, Permanent Secretary and Senior Administrative Officer.

During her public service career, Mrs. Bain-Thomas participated in and contributed to several public sector reform initiatives including the Value for Money studies, the training for the introduction of a new Performance Appraisal System, and proposals for the regulation of private practice for medical personnel in the Public Service. She was involved in the re-organization of the Ministries of Social Development and Carriacou and Petite Martinique Affairs, the strengthening of the Cabinet Office, and securing of training for senior managers of the Public Service.

Mrs. Bain-Thomas has served as a Director on the Board of Directors of several organizations and is an Accredited

Director. She is the Author of the book Unconstitutionally Removed.

As an Independent Contractor, Mrs. Bain-Thomas undertook several short-term consultancies and projects which included the development of a communications and a human resource policy for local institutions.

Mrs. Bain-Thomas has attended several short-term training courses in areas of human resource development, strategic and corporate planning, and project management. She is the holder of a B.Sc. in Public Administration and Law from the University of the West Indies, Cave Hill, Barbados; an LLB from the University of Wolverhampton, London, England, and an MBA in International Business from St. George's University, Grenada.

## Ms. Shanise Hutchinson

Hailing from the beautiful Island of St. Vincent and the Grenadines, Ms. Hutchinson is a 2022 graduate of The University of the West Indies (UWI), St. Augustine, Trinidad and Tobago. She holds a degree in BSc. Management and Economics (Double Major), First Class Honours. One of her favourite courses during her tenure at UWI was ECON 3052: Fiscal Policy and Economic Development. Since then, Ms. Hutchinson has been working part-time in the capacity of an economic Research Assistant focusing on fiscal policies within the Caribbean region. She enjoys reading for leisure, travelling, and experiencing new adventures, cultures, and food.

We appreciate the comments and suggestions from all the readers of Budget Alert.